Cambridge Elements

Elements in Translation and Interpreting
edited by
Kirsten Malmkjær
University of Leicester

TRANSLATING HIS-STORIES

Mª Carmen África Vidal Claramonte
University of Salamanca

Shaftesbury Road, Cambridge CB2 8EA, United Kingdom

One Liberty Plaza, 20th Floor, New York, NY 10006, USA

477 Williamstown Road, Port Melbourne, VIC 3207, Australia

314–321, 3rd Floor, Plot 3, Splendor Forum, Jasola District Centre,
New Delhi – 110025, India

103 Penang Road, #05–06/07, Visioncrest Commercial, Singapore 238467

Cambridge University Press is part of Cambridge University Press & Assessment,
a department of the University of Cambridge.

We share the University's mission to contribute to society through the pursuit of
education, learning and research at the highest international levels of excellence.

www.cambridge.org
Information on this title: www.cambridge.org/9781009673174
DOI: 10.1017/9781009673150

© Mª Carmen África Vidal Claramonte 2025

This publication is in copyright. Subject to statutory exception and to the provisions of relevant collective licensing agreements, no reproduction of any part may take place without the written permission of Cambridge University Press & Assessment.

When citing this work, please include a reference to the DOI 10.1017/9781009673150

First published 2025

A catalogue record for this publication is available from the British Library

ISBN 978-1-009-67317-4 Hardback
ISBN 978-1-009-67316-7 Paperback
ISSN 2633-6480 (online)
ISSN 2633-6472 (print)

Cambridge University Press & Assessment has no responsibility for the persistence or accuracy of URLs for external or third-party internet websites referred to in this publication and does not guarantee that any content on such websites is, or will remain, accurate or appropriate.

For EU product safety concerns, contact us at Calle de José Abascal, 56, 1°, 28003 Madrid, Spain, or email eugpsr@cambridge.org

Translating His-stories

Elements in Translation and Interpreting

DOI: 10.1017/9781009673150
First published online: October 2025

Mª Carmen África Vidal Claramonte
University of Salamanca

Author for correspondence: Mª Carmen África Vidal Claramonte, africa@usal.es

Abstract: Following Hayden White and the critical historiography of the 1960s, the idea underlying this Element is that a historical text is a translation of past events. This implies that retelling stories can vary depending on the historian/translator who recounts the facts. *Translating His-stories* focuses on how women – Jen Bervin, Patience Agbabi, Caroline Bergvall, Erin Mouré, and many others – dare to translate stories previously told by men. In line with contemporary theories of translation, these stories are translations because women rewrite, *again* but *for the first time*, what has already been told.

Keywords: translation, history, literature, feminism, fairy tales

© Mª Carmen África Vidal Claramonte 2025

ISBNs: 9781009673174 (HB), 9781009673167 (PB), 9781009673150 (OC)
ISSNs: 2633-6480 (online), 2633-6472 (print)

Contents

	Introduction	1
1	Historical Texts as Translations of the Past	2
2	Literature That Translates History	11
3	Overcoming the Danger of a Single Story: Women's Translations of Literary His-stories	17
4	Twice Upon a Time: Translating Children's Literature Again for the First Time	24
5	Women's Translations of Men's Literature	34
6	(Un)concluding Remarks	54
	References	58

Introduction

In *The Book of Embraces*, Eduardo Galeano (1989/1992: 118) cites an African proverb that states, "Until lions have their own historians, histories of the hunt will glorify the hunter." This Element is based on the firm belief that for many centuries History has been written by the hunters. Today this statement is widely accepted, after "critical historiography" finally deconstructed the idea that History is the objective and neutral narration of the events that occurred in the past.

Examples that history is anything but neutral are endless. For instance, visions of the Spanish Civil War radically differ depending on whether we read Paul Preston or Luis Suárez. The same also applies to what happened in 1492 when Christopher Columbus arrived in America, as in Isabel Wagemann's exhibition *Conquistadoras* (Madrid, Casa de América, October 2022– January 2023).[1] Examples are infinite, although one of the most extreme cases is doubtlessly that of those historians who deny the Holocaust.

Translating His-stories stems from the idea that revisionist narratives are crucial for any shift to happen.[2] The first section focuses on contemporary theories of critical historiography, which argue that the historical text is one way of translating reality, and that the historian is a translator. Accordingly, the historical text is thus understood as one narrative of facts among many other possible narratives. Without denying factuality, this view moves away from earlier theories such as the Rankean vision of history, which regarded the historical text as neutral and objective. Instead, it is an example of what Salman Rushdie (1981/1995: 459) calls "a chutnification of history."

Section 2 offers many examples of literary works that rewrite historical events previously told by dominant voices, such as Julian Barnes's *A History of the World in 10 ½ Chapters* (1989) or Elena Poniatowska's *La noche de Tlatelolco* (1971), among many others. The next section looks at how women have overcome what Chimamanda Adichie calls the danger of a single story, and have translated, for example, classic myths to tell hitherto untold stories. Section 4 addresses a very specific type of literature, the translations that women have made of well-known fairy tales in order to transform them into different stories devoid of any patriarchal bias. These new stories warn us that the protagonists do not always have to be blonde and blue-eyed, and that the end of the story is not always "and they lived happily ever after." In the final section

---

[1] www.casamerica.es/exposiciones/conquistadoras.
[2] An excellent example is what Baer (2020) calls the mythistory of Translation Studies, meant to open a space for heterogeneity in the field and to recognize the rhizomatic nature of its historical inquiry.

I examine the feminist translations of canonical authors such as William Shakespeare, Geoffrey Chaucer, or Fernando Pessoa, made by women writers, namely, Jen Bervin, Patience Agbabi, Caroline Bergvall, and Erin Mouré.

This Element argues that it is urgent to reread, rewrite, translate, and rethink all those stories that have been told from a single patriarchal point of view. In this context, this Element focuses on how women dare to be lionesses and rewrite stories previously told by men. In line with contemporary theories of translation, these stories are understood here as translations because women rewrite, *again* but *for the first time*, what has already been told.

1 Historical Texts as Translations of the Past

Following Hayden White in *Metahistory* (1975), the idea underlying this Element is that the historical text is one way of translating reality, and consequently, that the historian is a translator. Again, in another key text, *The Content of the Form* (1987: 1), White defines history as "the problem of how to translate knowing into telling." The historical text shows who produces knowledge and what are the politics of the production of a particular knowledge and on what basis certain contexts are foregrounded over others (Mohanty 1991: 3). Historical writing is seen as translating between different mediums (LaCapra 1983/1994: 26), where the past is converted into written form and interpreted through contemporary concepts (Jenkins 1991/2003: 15–16), as argued by Margarita Savchenkova, the editor of a special issue of *Translation Matters* on history as translation. In this context, historians act as translators bridging the past and the present. As Peter Burke (2005: 3) aptly states, "If the past is a foreign country ... then historians may be regarded as translators between past and present."

Taking critical historiography as my theoretical foundation, this section will approach historical texts as translations of the past, as intralingual translations[3] of past events, in line with some of the previously mentioned historians and many others (Alonzi 2024, 2023a, 2023b, 2023c). Retelling History (in the singular and with a capital H) is crucial because only in this way can other stories be heard, stories that have been silenced for centuries. The second half of the twentieth century was a period marked "by a tremendous multiplicity of discussions and innovations in historical writing and theory" (Olsen 2014: 1). In this Element I will concentrate on the views offered by the critical historiography of the 1960s, whose new conceptualizations and transgressing of the boundaries of mainstream historical writing gradually made clear that historical texts are translations of events. This means that rewritings of history can vary,

---

[3] For other types of intralingual translations see Pillière and Berk Albachten 2024.

depending on the historian who recounts the facts, the making of the historian. What has been called the making of the historian refers to how "the construction of historical writing goes hand in hand with the construction of scholarly identities and positions" (Olsen 2014: 4).

At the beginning of the twentieth century, the attack on historical realism highlighted the need to reflect on the misrepresentation that originates from the person telling the story: "'[T]he story' in history is provided by the historian" (Munslow 2013: 6). So, he argues that history is fundamentally "the process of translating evidence into facts" (Munslow 1997: 6) and is essentially "a translation exercise" (Munslow 2012: 150). The social sciences, Marxism, the beginning of the Indian "Subaltern Studies," the macro approach of the French Annales School or the micro approach of the Italian microhistorians, for example, subvert the Rankean view of history, that defended the idea that history is an objective, neutral discipline that gives a single account, the only true one, of events that took place in the past. The *Journal of the History of Ideas* (1940) and Walter Benjamin's *Theses on the Philosophy of History* (1955) along with other scholarly publications raised serious doubts that history is universal, unique, objective, and neutral. Questioning the objectivity of history is a first step, but a very important one.

Historians such as Hayden White, Dominick LaCapra, Michel de Certeau, Paul Veyne, Peter Burke, Louis O. Mink, Lionel Gossman, David Carr, Maurice Mandelbaum, W. H. Dray, Louis Mink, Nöel Carroll, and Frank Ankersmit no longer accepted the idea that the activity of the historian is to objectively discover and reconstruct the past. As they began to revise conventional historiographic notions such as objectivity, neutrality, transparency of representation, and impersonality, they progressively distanced themselves from a view of history as factual representation and preferred to understand it as a process of experimentation (LaCapra 2004, 2013; Munslow 2013). History thus became as "a deeply problematical concept" (Young 1990: vi), given that it is based on who decides what to tell or what to silence depending on one set of interests or another: "To the question 'What is history?', we must always add: 'Who decides? On what grounds, and to what end?'" (Morley 1999/2002: 23).

Undoubtedly, facts exist.[4] However, without denying factuality, it is no less true that the way we narrate facts does not change factuality but rather how facts are interpreted and how they are presented to the readers. Historical texts are narratives (Harding 2022a, 2022b) that tell stories (Bal 2009). They are a type of organized discourse that has undergone a process of selective appropriation

---

[4] This idea aligns with the Aristotelian concept of non-contradiction, which has been addressed in relation to research data (Mellinger and Hanson 2022).

(Baker 2006). History as a construction of narratives around events can also be a way of approaching contemporary events, as Harding (2012) has brilliantly shown in her analysis of Russian and translated reporting of the Beslan hostage-taking in 2004. Yet, even here, reports were written and published online after events have occurred,

> and Putin's televised address to the nation on the day after the bloody end of the siege, in which he recounted his history of the demise of the Soviet Union and the need for Russia to stand firm against further disintegration, is a clear example of how quickly the present becomes the past and can be ossified into a fixed, official narrative of "what happened and why", the very stuff of historiographical inquiry and anxiety.
>
> That Putin has the reach, power, and intention to ossify the history of Beslan, in spite of the efforts of local civil society to forge an alternative history ... demonstrates the importance of the narrator – including translators – in the writing of history. (Harding 2022a: 60)

Translation is a Foucauldian discursive practice (St-Pierre 1993) which urges us to ask how facts are transformed through translation and under what conditions that transformation is achieved. For instance, as Vicente Rafael argues in an interview with Christopher Rundle, translation is crucial in the workings of colonial history and in general in the formation of historical imagination. Translation opens the field to tell "a different history":

> From the perspective of histories of the relationship between self and society, or society and the State, translation is this generalized process differentiation - from within as well as across languages and societies, the study of which *allows us to get beyond historicist accounts of institutions and 'big men'*". (Rafael in Rundle and Rafael 2016: 26)

This approach *from below* makes the translator work "with the materiality of texts and the landscape of documental evidence to show how historical investigation will always be linked to the workings of translation in one form or another" (Rafael in Rundle and Rafael 2016: 29. See also Rundle 2020). So, the fact that colonized cultures have kept some words without translating them into the language of the colonizer has to do with what Rafael calls the insurgency of language:

> There is always resistance. There is the permanent possibility of a war of meaning against those who seek to use translation to prop up structures of power ... Translation does not convey meaning whole and untouched; rather it inflects and distorts it, leaving it open-ended, hence, available for on-going revision, subversion and supplementation ... There is in the very working of untranslatability the hope for some other possibility to emerge apart from

dominant structures of power. But there is also the risk that it may not, and what happens is that a more sophisticated, more penetrating and more comprehensive set of power relations emerge. (Rafael in Rundle and Rafael 2016: 33)

Until recently, History had always been told from what Hayden White (1987: 20) calls the "doxa" of the "historiographical establishment" (see also White 1978a: 46–47). This perspective endeavored to make the general public believe that historical discourse was unbiased, and that the story was a mirror image of the facts. However, ideology understood as "meaning in the service of power ... highlights the role language plays in establishing and sustaining sociohistorically situated relations of domination" (Knowles and Malmkjær 1996: 44). What occurred thus becomes a construction, where truths are "'useful fictions' that are in discourse by virtue of power (somebody has to put and keep them there) and power uses the term 'truth' to exercise control: regimes of truth" (Jenkins 1991/2003: 39).

Understanding a narrative as a construct means comprehending it from the perspective of a certain author and their view of what happened (Knowles and Malmkjær 1996: 47–49). A particular vision of a particular reality is conveyed through the author's choice of words and sources. History, like translation and writing in general, are signification systems we use to construct the meaning of the past:

> Historiography (that is, "history" and "writing") bears within its own name the paradox – almost an oxymoron – of a relation established between two antinomic terms, between the real and discourse. Its task is one of connecting them and, at the point where this link cannot be imagined, of working *as if* the two were being joined ... From this standpoint, reexamination of the historiographical operation opens on the one hand onto a political problem (procedures proper to the "making *of* history" refer to a style of "making history") and, on the other, onto the question of the subject. (de Certeau 1975/1988: xxvii)

The histories we assign to things and people are constructed, created, constituted and always conditioned by their context, Alun Munslow remarks in his preface to Keith Jenkins's *Re-thinking history* (1991/2003: xi). Thus, historians "carry out their translations of the past" (Alonzi 2023c: 667).[5] The narration thus becomes a semiotic representation, a translation, a rewriting told from the perspective of the dominant power. "Historical interpretation of the past can be considered an act of translation, epistemologically and cognitively" (Alonzi

---

[5] " ... the cognitive and linguistic processes through which historians perform their work always imply a translation of the different meanings of a past word/concept with the current meanings of that word/concept" (Alonzi 2023b: 670).

2023a: 1). Alonzi goes on to say something that is key to this Element: "This act of translation is also an act of synchronization which connects past, present, and future, disrupting and resetting time, as well as creating complex temporalities differing from linear chronology" (Alonzi 2023a: 1). For Alonzi (2024: 381), the task of the historian and that of the translator are similar:

> the act of translating is a creative act that is repeated every time that a "text" is translated. Every time that a text is translated, the translator gives it new life, thus enabling the translator's linguistic community to understand it with new words and to appropriate it; otherwise, the reason for continually retranslating texts would be incomprehensible. This is, in general, an exact description of the work performed by the historian when confronting past languages.

So, also in tune with the new, broader concept of translation in contemporary translation studies, we shall see how retelling stories already told by the dominant power means transferring them to other contexts, telling them in other words and in the voices of those who until now have been silenced. As Cronin (2007: 254) states in another context, we should ask not only what gets translated but also why so much is not translated.

In line with the contemporary view that "the boundaries of our discipline are expanding and blurring, with ever more interdisciplinary research, and definitions of translation becoming ever more amorphous and figurative so that they now often include any change or transformation from one mode to another" (Harding 2022a: 54), the idea underlying *Translating His-stories* is that translating is a dynamic and complex process that goes beyond the mere substitution of one language for another. The examples offered in this Element will show that translation is "a creative literary activity, for translators are all the time engaging with texts first as readers and then as rewriters, as recreators of that text in another language" (Bassnett 2006/2007: 174). They will show that words in translation "can shape our vision of the real and cause us to experience reality differently ... the translator as agent of metamorphosis may not only effect change but become himself or herself metamorphosised in the process" (Cronin 2007: 271).

Contemporary studies on translation are aware of the need to examine in depth the relationship between the production of knowledge in a given culture and its transmission, relocation, and reinterpretation in another context. The production of knowledge is mediated; it has to do with the production and ostentation of power and with the strategies used by this power to represent the other. This is all the more true of historical knowledge:

> But most heavily mediated is knowledge gained in the domain of translation history ... historical studies on translation depict sites of vigorous

contestations. They show how overdetermined works of translation often are –by the producers of grand narratives of national identity as much as by marginalized groups, hybrid groups, and by invaders, explorers, travellers, colonial administrators, missionaries, linguists, anthropologists, spies, and other such information-gatherers. (Cheung 2012: 156, 157)

The first step is to assume that there is not just one History but many, because stories are texts that depend on the words (White 1987) and sources that we choose. Far from being an objective activity, narrating, like translating, is a selective task. And that selection is made with words. Narrations are literary artifacts (White 1975, 1978a, 1978b). Whoever narrates history is a translator of facts, who must take into account the many ways in which the production of historical narratives reveals the asymmetry between groups and individuals who have very different access to the means of production of history (Trouillot 1995: xix).

Narrating thus becomes a first intralinguistic translation. In *Metahistory* (1975: 129), Hayden White explicitly states that the historical text is one way of translating reality, and consequently, the historian is a translator and, as mentioned earlier, in *The Content of Form* (1987), history is defined as a way "to translate knowing into telling" (White 1987: 1). In this same line, historian Reinhart Koselleck (2002: viii) considers that the history of historiography is a history of the evolution of the language of historians. History is thus "an act of translation" (Jenkins 1991/2003: 48). In this context, Hayden White asserts that history is a very effective way of developing self-reflection. Once again, it is not a matter of denying factuality but rather of putting facts on the table that have various interpretations and rewritings, and these rewritings are different ways of telling them.

Apart from Hayden White, the idea that history (or stories) is the construction of a narrator has also been observed by Roland Barthes, who in "The Discourse of History" (1967/1989) asserts that history is born of a narrator, which gives rise to the illusion of objectivity: "Presenting a story as if it is telling itself creates what Barthes called a 'referential illusion', an impression of objectivity ... objective discourse brings about a 'reality effect', the impression that the words match external referents" (Hermans 2022: 12).

As Spivak (1993/1996: 25) states, "History is, after all, a storying." She understands history as "history-writing" in her groundbreaking 1985 article "Subaltern Studies: Deconstructing Historiography" (Spivak 1985). Historians as translators relocate words and objects, words as objects, "words/objects of the present in the past; in this way they construct 'possible' stories/histories. It is like a circle that starts from the present, enters the past and returns to the present, all the while with a view to the future" (Alonzi 2023b: 200).

The way a story is told, namely, the words that are chosen and their arrangement in the sentence, gives rise to a type of narrative that alerts us to the urgency of not simply accepting the stories transmitted to us by those who in theory have the authority to do so. That is why we must ask questions about how those stories have been reconstructed, whom they represent, and why precisely the focus is on a certain group of people and not others. Many other questions must also be asked that in some circles will not be well received. Such questions not only force us to retrace our steps and follow the paths previously traveled by others but also to look for unusual, and perhaps unconventional, different, and uncomfortable ways out.

One of the literary works that best describes these new ways of seeing historical texts as translations of past events is *Haroun and the Sea of Stories*, where Salman Rushdie (1990/1999) introduces Rasid Khalifa, who lives in an extraordinarily sad city. Yet despite living in a city that has forgotten its name and whose factories produce, package and ship sadness, Rasid is a jovial man, perhaps because he is always telling stories. His son Haroun describes his father as a juggler, because the stories he tells are made up of bits and pieces of different stories that he handles as he pleases. When he asks his father where all these stories come from, Rasid discovers that they come from the Ocean of the Streams of Story. That place, the great Ocean of Stories, is really amazing, because it is full of the Streams of Story, a thousand and one different streams, each one of a different color. Furthermore, they are interwoven like a liquid tapestry forming an embroidery of enormous complexity, because each one of those strands of colors represents and contains a single story:

> ... Iff explained that these were the Streams of Story, that each coloured strand represented and contained a single tale. Different parts of the Ocean contained different sorts of stories, and as all the stories that had ever been told and many that were still in the process of being invented could be found here, the Ocean of the Streams of Story was in fact the biggest library in the universe. And because the stories were held here in fluid form, they retained the ability to change, to become new versions of themselves, to join up with other stories and so become yet other stories; so that unlike a library of books, the Ocean of the Streams of Story was much more than a storeroom of yarns. It was not dead but alive. (Rushdie 1990/1999: 72)

This is precisely what critical historiography and the later historiographic currents of the twenty-first century propose in a much more arid way. Rushdie's inclusive Sea may be seen as the starting point of this Element. Understanding historical texts as translations of the past made by a historian helps us to understand that there is no single History (with a capital H and in the singular). Rushdie aims for a sea full of different kinds of stories, fluid stories that have the capacity to change, to become new versions of themselves, to join with other stories and to metamorphose into something different. In other words, stories that are open to plural interpretations and not only limited to those imposed by the hegemonic power of the winners.

Rushdie also warns us that it is not going to be easy to give everyone a voice. Indeed, about halfway through the novel we learn that someone has poured poison into those coastal waters of the Ocean of the Streams of Story. The waters are now filthy, and Haroun realizes that the poisons have altered the colors of the streams of stories, dulling and graying them. In front of the multicolor, the different points of view, the monocolor, the unique History:

> The poisons had had the effect of muting the colours of the Story Streams, dulling them all down towards greyness; and it was in the colours that the best parts of the Stories in those Streams were encoded. So the loss of colour was a terrible kind of damage. Worse yet, the Ocean in these parts had lost much of its warmth. No longer did the waters give off that soft, subtle steam that could fill a person with fantastic dreams. (Rushdie 1990/1999: 122)

Many colors, different voices, freedom. All this is dangerous, and Poison Blenders want to ruin it. In this line, it is worth reproducing the following fragment of the novel, because it summarizes perfectly the sense and feeling of what this Element wants to show in a rather less poetic way:

> "These are the Poison Blenders," ... "We must make a great many poisons, because each and every story in the Ocean needs to be ruined in a different way. To ruin a happy story, you must make it sad ... Now the fact is that I personally have discovered that *for every story there is an anti-story*. I mean that every story and so every Stream of Story- has a *shadow-self*, and if you pour this anti-story into the story, the two cancel each other out, and bingo! end of story..."
>
> "The world, however, is not for Fun," Khattam-Shud replied. "The world is for Controlling."
>
> "Which world?" Haroun made himself ask.
>
> "Your world, my world, all worlds," came the reply. "They are all there to be Ruled. And inside every single story, inside every Stream in the Ocean, there lies a world, a story-world, that I cannot rule at all. And that is the reason why." (Rushdie 1990/1999: 160–161)

Controlling individual stories means controlling the world. To erase different perspectives, to silence stories that are not the official one is to construct History, the dream of any dictator. So, in "Notes on Writing and the Nation," Rushdie argues:

> History has become debatable. In the aftermath of Empire, in the age of superpower, under the "footprint" of the partisan simplifications beamed down to

us from satellites, we can no longer easily agree on what is the case, let alone what it might mean. Literature steps into this ring. Historians, media moguls, politicians do not care for the intruder, but the intruder is a stubborn sort. In this ambiguous atmosphere, upon this trampled earth, in these muddy waters, there is work for him to do. (Rushdie 1997: 36)

In *Midnight's Children* Rushdie tells his views on History in terms of food, through Saleem's cooked up chutneys and his "chutnification of history" (Rushdie 1981/1995: 459). The taste of the chutney, we read in the novel, is more than an echo of a long-ago taste. It is that old taste itself, and it has the power of bringing back that past. Thus, the "chutnification of history" is a way to retrieve and interpret memory. On the last pages of the novel Saleem hopes that perhaps one day the world may taste the pickles of history:

What is required for chutnification? Raw materials, obviously -fruit, vegetables, fish, vinegar, spkes. Daily visits from Koli women with their saris hitched up between their legs. Cucumbers aubergines mint. But also: eyes, blue as ice, which are undeceived by the superficial blandishments of fruit – which can see corruption beneath citrus-skin; fingers which, with featheriest touch, can probe the secret inconstant hearts of green tomatoes: and above all a nose capable of discerning the hidden languages of what-must-be-pickled, its humours and messages and emotions ... at Braganza Pickles, I supervise the production of Mary's legendary recipes; but there are also my special blends, in which, thanks to the powers of my drained nasal passages, I am able to include memories, dreams, ideas, so that once they enter mass-production all who consume them will know what pepperpots achieved in Pakistan, or how it felt to be in the Sundarbans ... believe don't believe but it's true. Thirty jars stand upon a shelf, waiting to be unleashed upon the amnesiac nation ... One day the world may taste the pickles of history. They may be too strong for some palates, their smell may be overpowering, tears may rise to eyes; I hope nevertheless that it will be possible to say of them that they possess the authentic taste of truth. (Rushdie 1981/1995: 460, 461)

Chutnification is a form of hybridization which provides cohesion but emphasizing the multiplicity of the ingredients, "to change the flavour in degree, but not in kind" (Rushdie 1981/1995: 461). Saleem refers to each chapter as a "pickle," which are mixtures of different ingredients that mix together, exchanging flavors:

The pickles Saleem refers to are not cucumber pickles, but mixtures of different ingredients that mix together, exchanging flavors, and are then preserved. Saleem refers to each chapter as a "pickle:" "One empty jar ... how to end? Happily, with Mary in her teak rocking-chair and a son who has begun to speak? Amid recipes, and thirty jars with chapter-headings for names? (Rushdie 1981/1995: 550)

Pickling is both a preservative act and a creative one:

> The implications of the "impure" cook positioned as postcolonial hero/writer, the significance of his mysterious act of implosive self-sacrifice in the generation of his pickles, his acts of omnivorous ingestion or "swallowing the world", the choice of marginal pickles as central food offering, and Saleem's insistence on the permeable nature of his cooking are not unrelated aspects; they are interconnected in how they speak back to a comprehensive way of looking at food and consumption in the culture. When seen as issuing from an "impure" cook, as connected to an act of self-sacrifice, as related to what Saleem has ingested or swallowed, and as an offering that is permeable or that "leaks", the use of pickling as central metaphor reveals a fresh articulation of the ethical and transformative role of art in the postcolonial context ... pickling is a dynamic and intentional act, which does not merely record the past but actively regenerates it to produce something new and improved. (Ray 2022: 64–65)

Saleem is the impure translator of the past, a hybrid being, a profane cook, an imperfect, impure and ambivalent creature who, unlike Brahmin, who cooks protecting himself against contamination, enjoys mixtures and pickling as "shadows of imperfection" (Rushdie 1981/1995: 529). This is the kind of chutnified stories we will see in the following pages, stories in which pickling "helps embody a multitudinous and diverse world" (Ray 2022: 75).

2 Literature That Translates History

Literature has adhered to these new critical currents of historiography, and there are now many writers who have decided to translate stories that have already been told in order to offer other views of past events. This section will offer a number of examples of literary works which follow these new critical ways of looking at history. These literary works will show that there are now many writers who have decided to translate histories intralinguistically, thus offering *again for the first time* new *translations* of stories that had already been told in order to offer other views of past events. These translations show how translating aspects of one culture into another "is never a simple semantic substitution. Rather, the self-images of two cultures come to bear on the matter and clash over it ... Translations, therefore, can teach us much about certain aspects of a culture at certain stages of its evolution" (Lefevere 1988: 26).

An extreme example of this is the world of *1984*, where "All history was a palimpsest, scraped clean and reinscribed exactly as often as was necessary. In no case would it have been possible, once the deed was done, to prove that any falsification had taken place" (Orwell 1949/1983: 39). In *1984*, Orwell (1949/1983: 213–214) announced that those who control the present control the past, and those who control the past control the future, and that history is not what happened but what historians tell us happened:

> "There is a Party slogan dealing with the control of the past," he said. "Repeat it, if you please."
>
> "'Who controls the past controls the future: who controls the present controls the past,'" repeated Winston obediently.
>
> "'Who controls the present controls the past,'" said O'Brien, nodding his head with slow approval. "Is it your opinion, Winston, that the past has real existence?"
>
> ...
>
> "No."
> "Then where does the past exist, if at all?"
> "In records. It is written down."

It is important that the other stories come to light, that reality be translated from other realities, and that these stories be narrated by the subalterns themselves (Chakrabarty 2002; Guha 1997). When Gayatri Spivak speaks of the subaltern in her essay "Can the Subaltern Speak?" (1988), she is not referring so much to the silence of the subalterns (Hindu women) or their inability to speak but to an unwillingness to listen to their voices. This is the case of *A History of the World in 10 ½ Chapters*, by Julian Barnes (1989), a novel in which the history of the world is accessed through the eyes of a termite. The termite is an insignificant creature, a "nobody" as Eduardo Galeano would say. It is also an entity with no symbolic capital in the words of Bourdieu, who speaks to us of "the story of the 'second' Noah" (Barnes 1989: 30).

History thus depends on who tells it. It can change by simply adding or removing a word, as demonstrated by José Saramago in his *História do Cerco de Lisboa* (1989). In fact, contemporary fiction frequently looks to specific historical figures to rewrite the hitherto official history. For example, Angela Carter rewrites the myth of Eve in *The Passion of the New Eve* (1977); Eduardo Galeano rewrites *Genesis* in *The Book of Embraces* (1989/1992); and Jen Bervin tells stories from the perspective of a worm in her *Silk Poems* (2017).

Many other novels approach history from a similar perspective. For example, in *The Chaneysville Incident*, by David Bradley (1981), John, the main character, relies on his narrative imagination to gradually go from being a historian to becoming a storyteller, which forces the reader to ask what the truth of history really is. In *Waiting for the Barbarians* (1980), Coetzee demonstrates how the habitus of the colonizer constructs the other (Spivak's "othering") to confirm his own reality. All of these novels and many others rewrite and translate history from the other's perspectives. For example, Graham Swift opens *Waterland* with this epigraph:

> *Historia*, ae, f. i. inquiry, investigation, learning. 2. A) a narrative of past events, history. B) any kind of narrative: account, tale, story. (Swift 1983: 1)

And a few pages further on, he describes historiography as a construct, in terms similar to those used by many contemporary historians:

> How many of the events of history have occurred ... for this or for that reason, but for no other reason, fundamentally, than the desire to make things happen? I present to you History, the fabrication, the diversion, the reality-obscuring drama. History, and its near relative, Histrionics. (Swift 1983: 34)

If in line with Hayden White and other historians, history is conceived as a narrative, it is hardly surprising that so many writers have reflected on what history means and how it represents the past, in other words, how it is constructed, reconstructed and translated, generally from the viewpoint of the conqueror. That is why many novelists have rewritten certain chapters of history, and some have even focused on rewriting world history in general. For this reason, history teacher, Tom Crick, the protagonist of *Waterland*, asks his students, " ... what is the point of history? Why history? Why the past?" And then he answers his own question by stating that history teaches us "to accept the burden of our need to ask why" (Swift 1983: 92, 93).

In the same way as many historians, novels such as *Shame* (1983) by Salman Rushdie, *Welcome to Hard Times* (1996) by E. L. Doctorow, *The Public Burning* (1977) by Robert Coover, and *A Maggot* (1985) by John Fowles, question concepts such as linearity and referentiality, not to mention representation, continuity, neutrality, and objectivity. They start from the idea that history narrates and constructs the past, and that the sources, archives, and texts from which historians create their history are, once again, nothing but representations.

Like Roa Bastos's narrator in *Yo, el Supremo* (1974), a historian is a compiler of discourses whose text is interwoven with many others. As Dominick LaCapra warns, no document is innocent. Instead, it processes and rewrites reality "in ways intimately bound up with larger sociocultural and political processes" (LaCapra 1985: 38). Thus, John Berger's *G.* (1972), Julian Barnes's *Flaubert's Parrot* (2009), and D. M. Thomas's *The White Hotel* (1981) question the status that traditional historiography has accorded to archives, and regard them as texts open to interpretation. In the case of Maxine Hong Kingston's *China Men* (1980), sequel to *The Woman Warrior* (1976), they can even be a collection of stories that tell the story of the men in her family.

Novels such as *Foe* (where Coetzee reinvents the story of Robinson Crusoe through Susan Barton, a castaway on a desert island) highlight the relationship between "story" and "history" and denounce the fact that the narrators of history have the power to silence and exclude events and stories of the past. They rightly claim that this is indeed what historians have always done throughout the ages (see Hutcheon 1988, 1989).

Other novels recount history from the perspective of the underdog. In Rudy Wiebe's *The Temptations of Big Bear* and Leonard Cohen's *Beautiful Losers*, the underdogs are the Canadian Indians, whereas in the novels of J. M. Coetzee, Toni Morrison, and Ishmael Reed, they are the blacks in South Africa and in America. Similarly in Paul Bowles's translations of the Moroccan writers and storytellers, Ahmed Yacoubi, Larbi Layachi, Mohammed Mrabet, or Mohamed Choukrim, the history of Tangier is told from the perspective of the oral storytellers who have always lived there (Vidal Claramonte 2023).

These are but a few of the many examples of what Linda Hutcheon calls "historiographic metafiction," or literature focused on revealing the ideological content of history as told by the victors.[6] Since the revision of history in historiographic metafiction does not distinguish between fiction and history, Linda Hutcheon (1989: 36) observes the following: "How do we know the past today? Through its discourses, through its texts – that is through the traces of its historical events: the archival materials, the documents, the narratives of witness ... the historian."

The literature that wants to retell the stories already told suggests that to re-enact the past is to open it to the present in order to prevent it from being a conclusive and teleological past. Novels like *Flaubert's Parrot* or *A Maggot* underline the fact that there is no single truth but many truths, no single order but diverse orders, each as arbitrary as the other – and if not, let us recall *Alphabetical Africa* or Walter Abish's *How German is It*.

All of them remind us that memory is not an instrument to explore the past but rather its representation. And these representations of the past obviously have ideological implications such as whom they belong to, and who constructed them. They also force us to reflect on the imposed nature of meaning, as reflected in novels such as *The Public Burning*. All writers are concerned "with memory, since all writing is a remembrance of things past; all writers draw on the past, mine it as a quarry. Memory is especially important to anyone who cares about change, for forgetting dooms it to repetition" (Greene 1991: 304).

---

[6] See Hutcheon (1988, 1989: 80–92) for an in-depth analysis of the treatment of archives in the historiographic novel.

Giving a voice to those who had no voice is empowering. Perhaps that is why Derrida asserts that Althusser's much-needed critique of the Hegelian concept of history and of the notion of expressive totality is aimed at demonstrating that there is not a single history or a general history, but rather different, scattered histories.

Indeed, there are many examples of contemporary writers who tell the stories of those who have been previously silenced. These range from Eduardo Galeano's "nobodies" (1989/1992) to the stories of subalterns in the case of *The Children of Sánchez* (1961/1970) by Óscar Lewis, or *La noche de Tlatelolco* (1971) by Elena Poniatowska. Both novels rewrite the official history taking as their sources the oral histories of its protagonists, the "nobodies." They are what Latin American literature calls *crónicas*, a form that emerged at the end of the 1960s whose aim was to narrate the plurality of voices of urban life and to record "a marginal reality, bringing to the fore aspects of city life that have tended to be ignored and articulating discourses from disempowered social groups" (Bielsa 2006: xiv).

La noche de Tlatelolco tells the massacre that took place on October 2, 1968, at the Plaza de las Tres Culturas, in Mexico D. F. This massacre is one of the subjects most studied by historians and explored by Mexican literature. Poniatowska does not tell History but stories, since she writes her *crónica* from the perspective of direct participants or witnesses and "shares an explicit commitment to denounce repression and abuse of authority, raise the consciousness of its readers about situations of political, economic, and cultural terror, and offer an alternative view to official, hegemonic history" (Jörgensen 1994: 68). The clash between the student movement and Díaz Ordaz's government is rewritten by Poniatowska by contrasting the official History about what took place and the voices of the conquered based on interviews, personal letters, diaries, recorded conversations and photographs which deny the construction of the facts as narrated by the official discourse. However, Poniatowska also decided to include the voice of those who opposed the student movement, and who represent a conservative, authoritarian discourse. The result is a multilayered text charged with heteroglossia and polyphony that challenges the authorized monochromatic version of what took place. Thus, she translates the official homogeneous History through many fragmented oral stories:

> She interviewed university and secondary students, parents, professors, workers, inhabitants of the Nonoalco-Tlatelolco housing complex, and other residents of the capital and foreign journalists ... Poniatowska visited the military camps and prisons where thousands of people were detained, and she accumulated other materials pertaining to the student movement ... The text that resulted from Elena Poniatowska's persistent research is a complex montage of many fragmented discourses. (Jörgensen 1994: 77)

These and other examples show that it is possible to *re*write the stories told by those in power if we *re*tell the stories that the powerful did not want to come to light. Why do we always remember 1492 but not 1493? As suggested by Julian Barnes in his, already mentioned, *A History of the World in 10 ½ Chapters*, we should celebrate 1493. This is the date of "the return, not the discovery" (Barnes 1989: 241), the date on which Christopher Columbus pocketed the 10,000 maravedis that he had promised to the first man who sighted the New World. The official history says nothing about the sailor to whom the money actually belonged. It had been won by a random sailor, but Columbus claimed it for himself, and as legend goes, the sailor then became a renegade. So, 1493 was also an interesting year. In line with many contemporary historians, Barnes (1989: 242) emphasizes that history is not what happened but what historians tell us happened:

> History isn't what happened. History is just what historians tell us. There was a pattern, apian, a movement, expansion, the march of democracy; it is a tapestry, a flow of events, a complex narrative, connected, explicable. One good story leads to another. First it was kings and archbishops with some offstage divine tinkering, then it was the march of ideas and the movements of masses, then little local events which mean something bigger, but all the time it's connections, progress, meaning, this led to this, this happened because of this. And we, the readers of history, the sufferers from history, we scan the pattern for hopeful conclusions, for the way ahead. And we cling to history as a series of salon pictures, conversation pieces whose participants we can easily reimagine back into life, when all the time it's more like a multi-media collage, with paint applied by decorator's roller rather than camel-hair brush.
>
> The history of the world? Just voices echoing in the dark; images that burn for a few centuries and then fade; stories, old stories that sometimes seem to overlap; strange links, impertinent connections . . . We think we know who we are, though we don't quite know why we're here, or how long we shall be forced to stay. And while we fret and writhe in bandaged uncertainty – are we a voluntary patient? – we fabulate. We make up a story to cover the facts we don't know or can't accept; we keep a few true facts and spin a new story round them. Our panic and our pain are only eased by soothing fabulation; we call it history. (Barnes 1989: 240)

These examples and many others show that translating History is, as stated at the beginning of this Element, much more than substituting one word for another. Translating a text means "reconfiguring it . . . No translation can ever be the 'same' as the original, for translation involves so much more than the linguistic, though obviously language is a crucial element . . . translators have to deal with more than just words which may or may not have dictionary equivalents" (Bassnett 2022c: vii). Translation is not a mechanical secondary act, but a complex process that goes beyond fidelity and equivalence. When translating History ethically, different narratives and counter-narratives are created (Baker 2006), thus extending the definition of translation and reflecting the values of horizontality, nonhierarchy, and pluralism (Baker 2016: 1).

These translations of History are examples of translation as a creative process that goes beyond an instrumentalist model, which conceives translation as reproduction, as a much more open territory, where translation is an interpretation that transforms a communicative artifact into something quite different. These and many other examples make clear that "the discipline has expanded so extensively that the term 'translation' can seem too narrow to reflect all that it encompasses ... [It is] a complex, multifaceted field of study, practice and theorization [... which] will continue to fascinate for the foreseeable future" (Malmkjær 2022: 1, 9). In this line, the next section will show translations as creative herstories. Creative herstories are creative translations in which

> meaning is as fleeting as the moment in which it arises and as unique and unrepeatable as the momentary constellation of participants in the relationship. It is therefore not repeatable whether in the same or another language; and that insight is liberating from the point of view of translation studies. There will never be sameness of meaning; but there may be coincidence, more or less close, of passing theories, in any instance of linguistic interaction. (Malmkjær 2020: 56)

3 Overcoming the Danger of a Single Story: Women's Translations of Literary His-stories

In this new context, and in line with Salman Rushdie's *Sea of Haroun* (1990/1999), where, as we saw, all stories wish to be told, a subversive and political translation of History is that offered by some women writers. This section will show examples of women who have rewritten stories previously told by men or who bring to light untold stories as translations of the stories previously told. Women thus become translators of the stories that have already been (un)told. Their translations have the capacity to become, as in Rushdie's current-filled sea, new translations which yearn to join other stories and to metamorphose into something different. Fortunately, throughout the twenty-first century stories have become increasingly hybrid and plural.

Women need to have the floor, because having a voice means expressing one's own point of view. It means beginning to have the power to deconstruct the homogeneous and supposedly universal foundations of patriarchal logocentrism:

> *Men dominate history because they write it*, and their accounts of active, brave, clever or aggressive females constantly tend to sentimentalize, to

> mythologize or to pull women back to some perceived "norm." As a result, much of the so-called historical record is simply untrue ... We also need women's history because so much of women's participation is frankly denied in the ceaseless effort to assert men's "natural" superiority at all costs. (Miles 1988/2001: 4, My italics)

Undoubtedly, there is danger when women begin to speak out. Today many women who realize that the story that has been told is not theirs have begun to rewrite the stories previously imposed by the patriarchy. These stories rewritten by women tell us for the first time again what has already been told. From a feminist perspective the centrality of rewriting and remembering history has always been recognized because "the very practice of remembering and rewriting leads to the formation of politicized consciousness and self-identity. Writing often becomes the context through which new-political identities are forged" (Mohanty 1991: 34).

Women's stories are rewritings that are open to many interpretations and are not only limited to those imposed by the hegemonic power of the victors. It is urgent to ask whose stories are told, from whose perspective and in whose voice. Whose stories, versions, and voices are left silent and on the contrary, whose are translated: "Whose tale will be told above and over all others as the official story? Whose voices will whisper around the edges of the canon, telling their heretical versions? Whose voices will be forcibly silenced, and whose will die out?" (Price 2004: xiii, xviii).

Women are aware of the power of telling, but especially of the power of telling a single story. In 2009, Chimamanda Ngozi Adichie stated that the single story creates stereotypes: "They make one story become the only story," and the single story "robs people of dignity." It is never accidental that those in power try to convince us that there is only one story:

> It is impossible to talk about the single story without talking about power. There is a word, an Igbo word, that I think about whenever I think about the power structures of the world, and it is "nkali". It's a noun that loosely translates to "to be greater than another". Like our economic and political worlds, stories too are defined by the principle of nkali: How they are told, who tells them, when they're told, how many stories are told, are really dependent on power. Power is the ability not just to tell the story of another person, but to make it the definitive story of that person. (Adichie 2009)

However, if we dare to reject the possibility that there is only one story, the one imposed on us, we can bring to light other stories that have been hitherto silenced, but which are also important:

> When we reject the single story, when we realize that there is never a single story about any place, we regain a kind of paradise ... Stories matter, many

stories matter. Stories have been used to dispossess and to malign, but stories can also be used to empower and to humanize. Stories can break the dignity of a people, but stories can also be used to repair that broken dignity. (Adichie 2009)

That is why Spivak (1993/1996: 27–28) stresses that it is not a matter of denying that truth exists but of questioning the stories that have been imposed on us. Or when constructing a narrative something is always left out, and it is not always obvious what (Spivak 1990: 9). The past is actually constructed histories, and none of them is the past but translations of the past: " ... we read the world as a text, and, logically, such readings are infinite" (Jenkins 1991/2003: 11).

Those who for centuries have been subalterns because they have had no voice now want to take the floor and breathe for themselves. As the Tobago-born poet Marlene NourbeSe Philip (2018: 38) writes:

What does it mean – breathing for an Other or Others? Or being breathed for? How is this affected by historical memory of enslavement? Do we ever re/present this act otherwise in our lives – on either side of the breath? And, more importantly, is there any significance to this act of radical hospitality within present day and historical contexts of systems of power that attempt to eradicate and erase the individual and those who are perceived as marginal, deficient, less than, and different? Many of us through gender, choice, or life situation will never physically breathe for someone else, but we have all experienced being breathed for.

By telling *again for the first time* what has already been told, women find themselves, not by taming words, but by letting the words keep their magic. As Sandra Gilbert points out, this is none other than accepting the possibility of going to sleep in one world and waking up in a different one. This can only happen if we question certainties and undermine foundations, to banish the dominant gaze in favor of the plural kaleidoscope. We must thus embark on a feminine journey that becomes a Derridean supplement to tell those other stories of women that for so many centuries have been silenced by those who have spoken for them:

We fear those who speak about us who do not speak to us and with us. We know what it is like to be silenced. We know that the forces that silence us because they never want us to speak, differ from the forces that say speak, tell me your story. (hooks 1991: 343)

Echoing stories already told, women tell them for the first time with a view to becoming the subjects, not the objects, of the discourse. Women translate the stories already told by the patriarchy from a feminine and feminist point of view. Their texts are translations that rewrite something for the first time. These rewritings paradoxically transform, in the Derridean sense of the word, the secondary into the primary. Women are translators of the first time again.

Women have embarked on a journey that revisits the road trodden in all disciplines. In the early 1980s, Craig Owens (1983) underlined the presence of an insistent feminine voice, and soon after, critical historiography gave way to books such as the *History of Women in the West*, coordinated by Georges Duby and Michelle Perrot (1991). Thanks to such contributions, the canon gradually became feminine and feminist, as reflected in literature with Elaine Showalter (1977) and her publication, *A Literature of Their Own*, and in art, with Linda Nochlin and Griselda Pollock, among others. Even in music, there is Susan McClary (1991/2002), who published *Feminine Endings: Music, Gender & Sexuality* in 1991. This feminist look from the "new musicology" of the seventies relates music to cultural studies, conceiving it as a type of discourse that has contributed to the creation of sexual stereotypes that can be deconstructed with a different interpretation of musical texts. Also interesting are the feminist rewritings of crime novels.

All of these books allow us to travel to other territories far from the falsely unitary founding subject, outside the great Lyotardian stories that theorists like Alice Jardine (1985: 24) describe as the crisis of the metanarratives invented by men. They revise myths and traditional stories and make revisions that are what Adrienne Rich refers to as "acts of survival." So now, *for the first time*, we can see the story translated, rewritten in other stories told by women.

Herstory began with mid-nineteenth century activists, such as Elizabeth Cady Stanton and Susan B. Anthony, who created a historical archive that was "different" from what was regarded as "universal." The result was an extensive collection of documents entitled *History of Woman Suffrage* (1881), which was largely ignored by most latter-day historians. In the same way, women's history was not taught in school and university classrooms because women lacked power and their ideas had never been taken into account. We seek a historiography that challenges generalization and that teaches us, as Chimamanda Adichie has observed, that there is no single story.

For centuries, women have been silenced by men, but now women are rewriting men's History in original stories. Contemporary feminist fiction recreates and rewrites classical voices from a perspective that reclaims and vindicates the voice of women. One of the best-known examples is Adrienne Rich, who in her poem "A Valediction: Forbidding Mourning" (1970) rewrites

John Donne's poem of the same title, and shortly afterward, speaks of the need to translate the past, or more specifically, of its re-vision in "When we Dead Awaken":

> We need to know the writing of the past, and know it differently than we have ever known it; not to pass on a tradition but to break its hold over us. For writers, and at this moment for women writers in particular, there is the challenge and promise of a whole new psychic geography to be explored. But there is also a difficult and dangerous walking on the ice, as we try to find language and images for a consciousness we are just coming into, and with little in the past to support us. (Rich 1972: 19)

An example is the 1980s genre of US black women's fiction "which collectively rewrites and encodes the history of American slavery and the oppositional agency of African-American slave women" (Mohanty 1991: 36). This is the case of *Beloved*, in which Toni Morrison rewrites and revises the history of slavery in the United States and of Gayle Jones's *Corregidora*, among many other examples.

Stories such as the myth of Eve are translated in Angela Carter's *The Passion of the New Eve* (1977). Also well-known is Jean Rhys's rewriting of *Jane Eyre* in *White Sargasso Sea* (2000), in which she translates the story of the "mad woman" from the viewpoint of a Dominican woman. In a different context, María Mercedes Carranza rewrites the silenced story of the silenced woman in Jan van Eyck's *The Arnolfini Portrait* (1434) in her 2004 poem "Aquí con la señora Arnolfini" [Here I am with Mrs. Arnolfini]. Michèle Roberts translates the story of Mary Magdalene in *The Wild Girl* (1984) and also retells the story of Noah's Ark from the perspective of Noah's wife in *The Book of Mrs Noah* (1987), whose ark on this occasion is filled with books and stories; likewise, she rewrites the life of Saint Teresa of Ávila in *Impossible Saints* (1997). More recently, Jane Crowther's *Gatsby* (2025) translates Jay Gatsby and Mick Carraway into women, Xiaolu Guo's *Call Me Ishmaelle* (2025) reimagines *Moby-Dick* from the perspective of a cross-dressed female sailor, and Sandra Newman's *Julia* (2023) offers a feminist version of Orwell's *1984*.

Women's translations of history are especially relevant in the case of their calling into question the stories of the ancient world. Women's stories are translations that are open to plural interpretations and are not only limited to those imposed by the hegemonic power of the victors. They exemplify Scott's (2006/2007: 116) idea that translation itself "is constantly redrawing maps, redisposing the territories of language and cultures." We shall see how women's translating does not merely register change "but actively works to produce it" (Scott 2006/2007: 116).

There are many rewritings of classical myths, such as Ursula K. Le Guin's *Lavinia* (2008), a new vision of Aeneas's wife, whom Virgil largely ignored. Also very well-known is Margaret Atwood's translations of mythic archetypes like Circe in the "Circe/Mud Poems" (*You Are Happy*, 1974) and her *Penelopiad* (2005), which tells the story of Odysseus from his wife's perspective and rewrites the women of the Odyssey in a feminist key (Estrada 2021). Similarly, Madeline Miller translates history in many of her novels. For example, in her *Circe*, it is not Odysseus who tells his story but Circe herself:

> My Circe is a feminist project. In Homer she is a character without relief. She does amazing things, but we don't know her motives. She turns men into pigs, but we are not told why. It is assumed that because she is a woman, she acts irrationally. Literary tradition presents her as an evil being who hates men, and it is assumed that she turns them into pigs as punishment, but in Greco-Roman tradition the pig has another symbolic value: it is related to sacrifices to the goddess, so Circe's motivations are much deeper, they are just never explained to us. (interview with Eduardo Lago in "Babelia," *El País*, 2 March 2019)

In *Cassandra*, Christa Wolf translates Homer's masculine epic and its wars in terms of the untold story of women and their daily lives,[7] whereas in her *Medea*, she gives a new slant to this classical myth (Bernstein 2020). These rewritings make clear that all translation:

> ... involves bringing something across both time and space. A text created in one cultural moment is then transformed into something offered to a new audience in a different cultural moment ... the very idea of "original" is called into question, for texts from the ancient world have been endlessly reshaped through transcriptions, copies, editions, commentaries and translations, they have been reconfigured through generations of different aesthetic and ideological criteria to the point where it is difficult, if not impossible, to determine what an original might be. Moreover, every translation is the product of one individual translator's interpretation, and that interpretation will have been shaped by the prevalent aesthetic and cultural norms of the time. (Bassnett 2022a: 240)

A particularly interesting example is Anne Carson, a poet whose work rewrites classical myths. Her poetry is an illustration "of the way in which translation can nourish the writing process, infusing the present with the emotions of another time ... her goal is to rearrange and disturb the meeting

---

[7] A very good example of a feminist translation of Cassandra in the art world can be found in Nalini Malani's *Can You Hear Me?*

of ancient and modern" (Simon 2007: 108). In fact, Carson's rewritings are sometimes startling:

> One of Carson's favourite procedures is to double up a classical author with a modern partner – Thucydides with Virginia Woolf as thinkers of war, Stesichoros (born 650 BC) and Gertrude Stein, as iconoclastic users of adjectives, those "latches of being", Simonides of Keos with Paul Celan. *Autobiography of Red* is a simultaneous telling of a Greek myth (the murder of Geryon by Herakles) and a modern tale of young love between a photographer and his boyhood lover, and their encounter later in life. (Simon 2007: 111)

In *Autobiography of Red* (1998), based on the Gerioneid of Stesichorus, Carson changes the story of Hercules and the monster Geryon by adapting it to contemporary times. Locating the story in Ontario, Canada and Peru, she also adds a queer perspective, by mixing a homosexual romance with Greek myth, since Geryon and Herakles are lovers. In *Nay Rather* (2013: 32) she takes a small fragment of ancient Greek lyric poetry and translates it "over and over again using the wrong words. A sort of stammering." Her translations are creative and feminist rewritings of the past (Bassnett 2022b). For instance, in *An Orestia*, the indefinite article of the title is a reminder that "this is not a translation of Aeschylus' Oresteia, it is Anne Carson's version of three plays by different playwrights about the tragic sequence of events concerning the cursed house of Atreus" (Bassnett 2022a: 246).

These examples and many others show that translation studies today has left behind narrow Eurocentric definitions of translation "as a univocal and unidirectional transfer of meaning from the source language to the target language, both of which are viewed as already polyvocal and hybrid" (Karpinski 2012: 4). In these translations "translation is transformative rather than imitative in that it makes the target language grow at the same time as it ensures survival of the original by making a foreign text perform new meanings in the target culture" (Karpinski 2012: 7, 8). A translation is understood here not as an act of preservation nor an act of recall "but an act of transmission (of handing on a text in what is deemed an appropriate form) and of reimagination … translation should seek to make the ST more incomprehensible, rather than preemptively predigesting it" (Scott 2006/2007: 108). Women's translations make "the ST more incomprehensible by making it progress through time" (Scott 2006/2007: 108).

There must be something dangerous in the fact that women speak and that their discourses proliferate, to use Foucault's words (1970/1981: 11). There are many women who, having understood that the story that has been told is not theirs, rewrite the stories that patriarchy has so far imposed. These stories rewritten by women tell again, for the first time, what has already been told. As women rewrite previously written discourses, they alert us to the fact that discourses can be both an instrument and an effect of power, but also a point of resistance.

In retelling for the first time what has already been told, women find themselves not taming words, but allowing them to maintain their magic, which is none other than the ability not to exclude. This will only be possible by questioning certainties and undermining foundations, in order to banish the dominant gaze in favor of the plural kaleidoscope.

4 Twice Upon a Time: Translating Children's Literature Again for the First Time

In both literature and art, women translate stories that have already been told. Now women at last take the floor. They now have a voice to tell stories that men had previously told for them. Feminist rewritings criticize the traditional binary opposition systems of the West. Through gender studies, many of the stereotypes created for women are now being demolished in an effort to transcend all essentialisms. These translated stories have the potential to become new versions of themselves, merge with other stories and become something completely different. Women's stories are thus open to multiple interpretations and are not limited to those imposed by the hegemonic power of the victors. From this perspective, translation has become a powerful vehicle for political, social and cultural change.

Of the many types of rewritings, this section focuses on feminist translations of traditional fairy tales.[8] Over the years, in children's literature, there have been numerous translations of History into herstories. However, it should be underlined that this type of literature is never neutral, but is always a vehicle for ideology (Knowles and Malmkjær 1996: 41–80).

There are many rewritings of classical stories that have been traditionally told throughout the ages.[9] According to Hasse (2004: vii), despite the existence of some previous work, scholarly research explicitly devoted to feminist issues in fairy-tale studies really began with Marcia K. Lieberman's "Some Day My Prince Will Come" (1972) and Sandra M. Gilbert and Susan Gubar's (1979)

---

[8] Importantly, the most classic fairy tales have their non-Western equivalents, which in many cases are the precursors of well-known fairy tales in the West (Haase 2010; Teverson 2019). For an analysis of fairy tales in Europe as well as in Africa, Asia, Australasia, and the Americas, see Teverson (2019).

[9] In the art world, examples of feminist interpretations of traditional stories can be found in the work of well-known artists such as Cindy Sherman, Paula Rego, Dina Goldstein, Kiki Smith, Natalie Frank, Helena Blomqvist, and Jona Jonas (for an analysis, see Slack-Smith 2018; Vidal Claramonte 2025). In a completely different context, also Taylor Swift has used fairy tales (Feder and Tatreau 2024).

provocative analysis of "Snow White" in *The Madwoman in the Attic* (see Joosen 2011: 215–297).

Since then, there have been hundreds of feminist rewritings of fairy tales (Guran 2016; Kérchy 2011), and retranslations of histories into herstories (Deane-Cox 2016). These rewritings have been analyzed in depth by authors such as Jack Zipes, Christina Bacchilega, Marian Warner, and many others. Thanks to their valuable insights, ideas about fairy tales have finally begun to change.

In their introduction to *Inviting Interruptions: Wonder Tales in the Twenty-First Century*, Bacchilega and Orme (2021) highlight some of the publications that contributed to us no longer seeing fairy tales as narratives "just for children," with no bearing on the ethical and gendered construction of the world of children. It was thanks to books like Jack Zipes's *Don't Bet on the Prince: Contemporary Feminist Fairy Tales in North America and England* (1987) that things began to change. This book was "a breath of fresh air, sampling stories by Margaret Atwood, Angela Carter, Anne Sexton, Tanith Lee, Jane Yolen, and others who were in different ways questioning and playing with dynamics of gender, genre, and power in classic fairy tales" (Bacchilega and Orme 2021: x). In the 1990s other highly relevant publications would appear, to widen the field of fairy-tale revisioning further.[10] These theoretical reflections along with many others[11] analyze the hundreds of rewritings of traditional tales in order to achieve what Angela Carter (1983: 24) proposes in "Notes from the Front Line": "I am all for putting new wine in old bottles, especially if the pressure of the new wine makes the bottle explode."

However, this is not the place for an in-depth study of other types of children's stories that are starting to appear in the twenty-first century which are not rewritings of traditional stories so much as narratives that attempt to bring young audiences closer to phenomena such as migrations.[12] Suffice it to

---

[10] "Ellen Datlow and Terry Windling's fairy-tale series with, for example, *Snow White, Red Blood* (1995) and *Black Swan, White Raven* (1997) and in Kate Bernheimer's collection *Mirror, Mirror, on the Wall: Women Writers Explore Their Favorite Fairy Tales* (1998). And in the twenty-first century so far, English-language edited collections of 'new fairy tales' include Bernheimer's *Brothers & Beasts: An Anthology of Men on Fairy Tales* (2007) and her literary anthology *My Mother She Killed Me, My Father He Ate Me: Forty New Fairy Tales* (2010); Stephen Jones's horror *Faerie Tales: Stories of the Grimm and Gruesome* (2013); *Sandra Beckett's Revisioning Red Riding Hood around the World: An Anthology of International Retellings* (2014); Paula Guran's *Once Upon a Time: New Fairy Tales* (2013) and *Beyond the Woods: Fairy Tales Retold* (2016); Dominik Parisien and *Navah Wolfe's Starlit Wood: New Fairy Tales* (2016), which gathers retellings of individual tales" (Bacchilega and Orme 2021: x).

[11] For an overview of the many possibilities that are opening up in the field of translation for young audiences, see Borodo and Díaz-Cintas (2025).

[12] Perhaps with the exception of *Little Red Riding Hood*, which was rewritten with migration as its starting point and adapted to contemporary migrations, see Pulliam (2025).

say that there are hundreds of stories that tell children about the experiences and hardships that refugee and migrant children are currently enduring in refugee camps or in countries that are foreign to them.

Still another type of modern story is that which deals with nontraditional families, such as *Mommy, Mama and Me* (2009), *Daddy, Papa and Me* (2009), or *Heather has Two Mummies* by Lesléa Newman, or Anna Membrino's *My Mums Love Me* (2022). Still other stories raise issues that until now have rarely been addressed, such as LGBTIQ+. This is the case of *Will Grayson, Will Grayson* (2011) by John Green and David Levithan, which has now become a classic. Also relevant here is the section titled "Regendering Cinderella" in Hennard Dutheil de la Rochere, Lathey, and Woźniak (2016: 143–254).

In this sense, *Freckleface Strawberry* (2007) by actress Julianne Moore is significant. This book was banned from schools in February 2025, just a few weeks after the beginning of Donald Trump's second term in office. Perhaps the reason for this absurd censorship is that the book celebrates difference. The story is about a girl who is a little different from the others because she has freckles. As the girl grows up, her freckles do not go away, and she learns that it is precisely in difference, not in homogeneity, that we are enriched as human beings. So, the story ends with the line "she lived happily ever after," a phrase that in this case has a different meaning from traditional stories. Clearly, difference, no matter how slight, frightens the powerful.[13]

The objective of these re-visions of traditional tales is to raise "awareness of the fairy tale as a primary site for asserting and subverting ideologies of gender" (Hasse 2004: 2). Accordingly, Anne Sexton's *Transformations* (1971) rewrite and transform tales by the Brothers Grimm with echoes of Betty Friedan's (1963) *The Feminine Mystique* and Tanith Lee's (1979) "Red as Blood" (1979). In the 17 tales that she translates, Sexton criticizes "And they lived happily ever after" by including contemporary references, acerbic humor, and feminism. Her stories do not take place in fantasy realms but in the sphere of everyday life, without the magic that supposedly makes life perfect. Instead she brings to light the problems of domestic life and the secondary role of women.

There is great interest in the rewritings of classic children's stories because this type of text is the one that most frequently stereotypes women in terms of the male gaze.[14] In practically all fairy tales, active and independent women are

---

[13] Julianne Moore is the author of other books for children, of which various are about Freckleface Strawberry. In another book, titled *My Mom Is a Foreigner, But Not to Me* (2013), she pays homage to all the Muttis, Mammas, and Mamans, who are from other countries and eat, speak, sing, and dress differently from other moms.

[14] One of the voices speaking out against this school of thought was that of Alison Lurie, who, in a controversial 1970 essay, "Fairy Tale Liberation" (*The New York Review of Books*, December 17, 1970, p. 42) argued the opposite. According to Lurie, fairy tales place women

bad and ugly, whereas good women are only beautiful. They are fragile, passive objects at the service of others (Bacchilega and Orme 2021: xi, xiii). This vision was summarized decades ago by Andrea Dworkin (1974: 48–49), one of the feminists most critical of fairy tales. According to her, these tales have only two definitions of women:

> There is the good woman. She is a victim. There is the bad woman. She must be destroyed. The good woman must be possessed. The bad woman must be killed, or punished. Both must be nullified... happiness for a woman is to be passive, victimized, destroyed, or asleep... It tells us that the happy ending is when we are ended, when we live without our lives, or not at all.

It is thus curious that the most well-known fairy tales in the Western world are those of Charles Perrault, the Brothers Grimm, and Hans Christian Andersen, even though the author of the first fairy tale was Baroness Marie Catherine d'Aulnoy. Written in 1690, her tale was about an independent fairy queen who did not need men. Sadly, the origin of the fairy tale has since been forgotten, possibly because it was not considered to be of interest.

One of the first women to criticize the patriarchal perspective in fairy tales and speak of its consequences was Luisa Valenzuela (1938), author of "La llave" [The Key]. In this story, she warns her readers:

> Hay que reconocer que empecé con suerte, a pesar de aquello que llegó a ser llamado mi defecto por culpa de un tal Perrault -que en paz descanse- el primero en narrarme. Ahora me narro sola.
>
> [Admittedly, I started out lucky, despite what came to be known as my flaw because of a certain Perrault – may he rest in peace – who was the first to narrate me. Now I narrate myself.]

Her words are meaningful because they trace the path followed by many women writers and artists, who have now begun to tell the stories that others had already told for them. For instance, "Little Red Riding Hood" has been rewritten many times from different perspectives. As previously mentioned, over ten years ago, Sandra Beckett (2013) published an anthology of international retellings of the tale, which revision Red Riding Hood throughout the world. The same has occurred and continues to occur with Cinderella (Hennard Dutheil de la Rochere, Lathey, and Woźniak 2016). There are also white, yellow, and green Little Riding Hoods –created by Bruno Munari– and punk versions of

---

in positions of power and represent the first step toward their liberation. One of the best-known responses to Lurie's article was that of Marcia Lieberman (1972) in her essay "'Some Day My Prince Will Come': Female Acculturation through the Fairy Tale" (for a detailed analysis of Lieberman's article, see Joosen 2011: 49–121). It is also relevant to mention the opposite position adopted, for instance, by writers such as Antonia S. Byatt, Iris Murdoch or Margaret Drabble, who argue that fairy tales have an application to the real world (Fiander 2004).

traditional fairy tales (Parrish 2021, 2019), among many other translations. The sheer abundance of this literature is eloquent proof that the feminist translations of traditional fairy tales[15] are very popular today.[16]

One of the best-known examples is Angela Carter's revisioning of Red Riding Hood in *The Bloody Chamber* (1979).[17] According to Sharon Deane-Cox (2016: 16), Carter's tale is an example of "retranslation" because *Cinderella: or the Little Glass Slipper* "deliberately differentiates itself from Samber [a nineteenth-century predecessor] in order to renew the meaning of Perrault's tale and its moral ... a renewal which ultimately allows the work to fully covey the feminist retranslator's own emancipatory message." Angela Carter had also translated Perrault in 1977, transcreating him (Hennard Dutheil de la Rochère 2019, 2013). Interestingly, these translations and transcreations were the first step toward her subsequent feminist rewrites of the stories:

> A few years later, Carter seized an opportunity to brush up her French when she was commissioned to retranslate *Charles Perrault's Histoires ou contes du temps passé, avec des Moralités* (1697) into English for Victor Gollancz. She deliberately modernized their language and message in *The Fairy Tales of Charles Perrault* before rewriting them for adults in *The Bloody Chamber and Other Stories*. Despite the linguistic, historical, and cultural gap, Carter found in *Perrault's contes* a type of imaginative literature compatible with her own "demythologizing" project. (Hennard Dutheil de la Rochère 2013: 2)

Jack Zipes's introduction to the Penguin reissue of *The Fairy Tales of Charles Perrault* (2008) highlights the importance of Carter's translation of Perrault in regard to her work. In fact, Carter not only made feminist translations of the stories but also multimodal translations since she experimented with fairy tales in her radio plays. Her radio plays were meant to recreate

> ... the aural experience of storytelling and explore "the atavistic lure, the atavistic power, of voices in the dark," with sound effects designed to stimulate the listener's imagination (or inner eye). The scripts were published in book form in *Come unto These Yellow Sands* (1985), with paintings by

---

[15] The feminist retelling of fairy tales has been the focus of countless studies (Bacchilega 1997, 2013, 2018; Bacchilega and Orme 2021; Bernheimer 1998, 2010; Guran 2013, 2016; Haase 2004, 2010, 2016; Harries 2001; Tatar 1987/2019, 1992, 2020, 2015; Warner 1995, 2014; Zipes 1986, 2000, 2001).

[16] In January 2025, just a few days after Donald Trump won the election again, Jeremy Harrison published a book whose title alludes to a typical phrase from fairy tales: *Mirror Mirror On The Wall: Donald Trump & A Reflection of FDR's Four Freedoms*. His choice of title is thought-provoking, to say the least.

[17] Carter's sexualization of women and her opinions on pornography, as reflected in her article "Polemical Preface: Pornography in the Service of Women" (Carter 2000) as well as in her fiction (i.e., *The Bloody Chamber*) have placed her in a complicated position with respect to many feminists and has generated rivers of ink.

Richard Dadd. Three of Carter's radio plays offer variations on "Puss in Boots," "Little Red Riding Hood," and "Sleeping Beauty" and hence rework the same fairy-tale material used in The Bloody Chamber. Each time the story is transposed into another medium, it produces an altogether different experience, whether as oral performance or written text. (Hennard Dutheil de la Rochère 2013: 6)

In this case, multimodal translations, which involve various senses, are set in motion.

Intermedial transposition, therefore, was a mainspring of Carter's creative enterprise not only because the writer experimented with her own work and the idea of the multiple, multidimensional, and open-ended text, but also because she had a strongly visual imagination and a long-standing interest in the interrelationship between text, voice, and image. (Hennard Dutheil de la Rochère 2013: 6)

Carmen Martín Gaite's *Caperucita en Manhattan* (1990) is a very different translation of Perrault's tale. It is an ode to freedom and the difficulty of achieving it. In this rewriting, Sara Allen lives in Brooklyn. Although she goes to Manhattan with her mother every Saturday to take her grandmother a strawberry cake, she dreams of being able to go by herself. One day when Sara Allen runs away from home to visit her grandmother, a former *music hall* singer who has lived a life without restrictions, she gets lost. On her timeless journey, she meets Edgar Wolf, a multimillionaire pastry chef who lives in a skyscraper in the shape of a cake. She also encounters Miss Lunatic, an ageless beggar who by day hides out in the Statue of Liberty and by night ventures out to mediate in cases of human misfortune. And sometimes, when necessary, she may even gift an elixir capable of conquering fear.

Of the many feminist translations of "Little Red Riding Hood," Niki Daly's *Pretty Salma. A Little Red Riding Hood Story from Africa* (2007) is also worth mentioning because it is so different. This is the African version of Little "White" Riding Hood, in which Pretty Salma's grandmother sends her to the market and warns her not to talk to anyone. Predictably, she disobeys and engages in conversation with the evil Mr. Dog. Set in Ghana, this rewriting, or "once upon a first and second time" of the new "Little Red Riding Hood," includes African words such as *ntama*, *Ka Ka Matobi*, and *Goema Goema*. Without forests or wolves, this intersemiotic and multimodal translation takes us on a journey through time and space, which rewrites the colors, images, clothes, food, and many other referents of the tale. As there are no wolves in Africa, Daly replaced the bad character with a dog because Africa has many dogs.

Still another critical response to traditional fairy tales is Buhle Ngaba's (2019) *The Girl without a Sound*, the story of a story that should have been told from the very beginning:

> The reactions they shared with me through the hashtag #BooksForBlackGirls confirmed my suspicions. I had known for a long time that there was a need for a book like this. If you go into a South African bookstore to buy something for children, you will notice that there are no books with little black protagonists. I wonder, how can we expect our children to see themselves and believe in their own magic if they are not represented in the stories they read?

Significantly, although the book can be purchased in paper format, the digital version is free when downloaded from the website. It is available not only in English but also in Setswana, one of the co-official languages of South Africa, which is spoken in Zimbabwe and Namibia, and by the majority of the population in Botswana. The new protagonists of the stories no longer have to be white and blonde, but can also speak in hitherto minoritized languages.

In *The Girl without a Sound*, Ngaba tells the story in English and in other minority languages such as Afrikaans, isiNdebele, Siswati, isiXhosa, isiZulu, Sepedi, Sesotho, Setswana, Tshivenda, and Xitsonga. Her story is of a black girl who has no voice because a golden cocoon grows in her throat. She thus represents the thousands of women, ignored and silenced by a racist and patriarchal society. A woman with red wings and sun rays on her skin will help her find her voice through books and words. Ngaba thus responds to traditional Western fairy tales, inhabited by white, blonde, and blue-eyed princesses, and always told in Western languages. As Ngaba writes:

> "The Girl Without a Sound" was born out of defiance and as a response to the fairytales we were told as little girls. Stories about white princesses with blue eyes, flowing locks of hair and an overwhelming awareness of their beauty. More than that, I want it to be a healing balm for all who read it. For the black female bodies that are dismissed or violated in a white, patriarchal and racist reality. As an act of restoring power and agency to young black girls in South Africa, I wrote a story about a voiceless girl of colour in search of a sound of her own. For it to be the catalyst that reminds them of the power of the sounds trapped inside them.

Another example is the Nigerian writer, Abi Daré, author of *The Girl with the Louding Voice* (2020). This a story is about girls who never receive an education because of poverty and gender discrimination. Daré speaks for those girls who are silenced yet who want to have a voice. The story is written in "broken English" because in this way, she thinks that the reader will be able to enter the story. Because she seeks a broader audience, Daré does not write in Yoruba.

However, standard English cannot convey the images, sounds, and smells that reflect her culture. That is why she explains that she has to "break" it. The result is striking but very difficult to translate. Nevertheless, her nonstandard English must also be translated because it transmits a subtle but important part of the meaning of the text:

> You see there's a thing when you're telling a story that a lot of people have heard, that people think, "OK, whatever it's just another story of another girl in poverty." I didn't want it to be that. I wanted people to listen. As a writer, it forced me to listen to Adunni. I wanted to make sure that every single thought of Adunni, every sight, every smell, everything she heard was well-recorded. I couldn't write it in Yoruba because that would just kill accessibility but I thought if I could at least break it down a little bit into nonstandard English, it's not pidgin English. It's her own voice, her own words. It forced me not to describe things in generic terms, not to use the same metaphors and similes that I was used to, that I learned in English language. I really wanted her story to be authentic, to be her own story. (Daré 2020)[18]

A different retelling is Babette Cole's *Princess Smartypants* (1986), who prefers her motorcycle, dragon friends, and independence to getting married. In *Prince Cinders* (1987), Cole introduces us to a new (male) Cinderella, who has three large hairy brothers and is forced to do all of the household chores. This feminist version of *Cinderella* tells the story for the first time, once upon a time, but from a different perspective than that of the male gaze.

Still another first time again can be found in the many existing Alices, a character that contrasts with the Victorian "Angel in the House" who has been a rich source for feminist literary criticism (for instance studies by Judith Little and Megan S. Lloyd[19]) since she defies the passive ideals of Victorian womanhood. Contemporary rewritings include Maeve Kelly's *Alice in Thunderland* (2002) or the head of Alice in Wonderland as seen from within by the viewer in Jaume Plensa's sculpture titled *Wonderland* (2013). A particularly interesting translation of the traditional Alice is Nancy Sheppard's aboriginal translation entitled *Alitji in Dreamland/Alitjinya Ngura Tjukurmankuntjala* (1992). Set in aboriginal Australia,

> White Rabbit becomes a White Kangaroo. Billy Tea and Damper party replace the Mad Tea-party. Game of croquet is now Game of the Witch Spirit ... There is no Pitjantjatjara word for "rabbit" (as these species were brought to Australia by the white settlers) so, naturally, Alitji sees a white kangaroo instead (yes, white as snow kangaroos do exist). The Caterpillar

---

[18] https://assembly.malala.org/stories/abi-dari-interview
[19] A more critical perspective is offered by Garland 2008. For a study of the unresolved conflicts surrounding whether Carroll's novel is a feminist text see Shi 2016.

becomes a Witchety Grub, the pepper in the "Pig and Pepper" chapter becomes the native itunypa plant, while the baby changes not into a pig but a native Australian bandicoot.[20]

The book is presented in two languages, and each page has the text in both languages – Pitjantjatjara and English.[21] In this multimodal text, as in most children's literature, images are as important as the text. Donna Leslie, a First Nations woman of the Gamileroi people, translates this Alice visually, through illustrations whose colors, forms, and bodies are completely different from the traditional Western ones.[22]

What Bacchilega and Orme call "wonder tales" is a comprehensive term for the moment in which now we find ourselves, where publications such as their own edited volume or the *Routledge Companion to Media and Fairy-Tale Cultures* (Greenhill et al. 2018) invite us to continue translating these tales, to include all possible voices, and "to consider media studies, eco-criticism, disability studies, and Indigenous studies as relevant to your understanding of wonder tales" (Bacchilega and Orme 2021: xix).

The examples that continue to emerge with the advance of the twenty-first century reveal the urgent need to translate these stories for the first time again through a feminist lens instead of through the traditional male gaze. If afterward, we make interlinguistic translations of that first translation that rewrote History into herstories, the elements in these new translations should still allow readers to glimpse the "original" text while at the same time giving it a new reading. For example, Snow White's seven dwarfs can be transformed into the most diverse characters:

> from seven jazz musicians (Fiona French, *Snow White in New York*), seven hippies (Uta Claus, *Total tote Hose*), seven partisans (Iring Fetscher, "Das Ur- Schneewittchen"), seven friars (Regina Doman, *Black as Night*), and seven exploited miners (Mary Maher, "Hi Ho, It's Off to Strike We Go!") to seven aliens (Laurence Anholt, *Snow White and the Seven Aliens*) and seven giraffes. (Gregory Maguire, *Leaping Beauty*) (Joosen 2011: 15. For other rewritings of Snow White, see Sohár 2019.)

Publishers have also realized the importance of these rewritings. Vintage, for example, published its *Feminist Fairy Tales* series, consisting of four rewritings

---

[20] Natalia Bragaru www.kidsbookexplorer.com/alitji-in-dreamland-alitjinya-ngura-tjukurmankunt jala-nancy-sheppard-donna-leslie/.

[21] "The indigenous language of 'Alitji' – Pitjantjatjara – is one of the few hundred languages spoken by the Aboriginal peoples inhabiting parts of South Australia, Western Australia and the Northern Territory" (Natalia Bragaru www.kidsbookexplorer.com/alitji-in-dreamland-alitjinya-ngura-tjukurmankuntjala-nancy-sheppard-donna-leslie/).

[22] For a detailed analysis of Indigenous wonder tales, see ho'omanawanui 2018.

by important authors such as Rebecca Solnit, Malorie Blackman, Jeanette Winterson, and Kamila Shamsie, who have created "fairy tales reimagined for modern boys and girls – transformed into stories of liberation that don't need a happily ever after." In fact, some of these rewritings have enjoyed unprecedented editorial success, such as *Good Night Stories for Rebel Girls* by Elena Favilli and Francesca Cavallo (2016). Despite the criticism received (Castro and Spoturno 2021: 230–234), its success has been confirmed by its many literary awards and its translations into almost fifty languages.[23]

Likewise, Disney has also attempted to update fairy tales, whether for ethical reasons or for purely economic ones. For this reason, many of its most emblematic characters (not just princesses) have evolved considerably. Nevertheless, in many cases, this apparent translation of traditions fails to convince, perhaps because at a deeper level, the "Disneyfication" of fairy tales continues.[24] In the Disneyization[25] process, the source material is sugarcoated and any real-life problems are eliminated in order to appeal to mass audiences (Leduc 2020; Wright 2016). This is typical of Western society, grounded in consumerism (Bryman 2004; Holliday 2019; Whelan 2014). There is also the fact that in many cases, Disney surreptitiously continues to perpetuate traditional stereotypes:

> From 2014 to 2023, The Walt Disney Company launched two princess live action adaptations (Maleficent 2014; *Maleficent: Mistress of Evil* 2019) and five remakes (*Cinderella* 2015; *Beauty and the Beast* 2017; *Aladdin* 2019; *Mulan* 2020; *The Little Mermaid* 2023). Compared to the animated classics originally produced between the 1950s and 1990s, these re-imaginations are made not just bigger – with new CGI technology, star castings and fancy costumes – but better, updating the princess characters with modern feminist ideas and vocabularies ... all remakes centralize the princesses' resistance against patriarchy and end on their dual triumphs of marrying a respectful prince (except Mulan) and overcoming initial restrictions, touching on popular feminist ideals of aspiration, independence, empowerment and having it all. However, these strategic

---

[23] Olga Castro and María Laura Spoturno (2021) is an excellent analysis of the reception in Spain and Argentina of the Spanish translation of this book, which discusses the differences between these two contexts.

[24] " ... the Disney fairy tale promises to fulfill what is lacking in our lives, to compensate for discomforting aspects of social reality, and to eliminate social and class conflicts forever. It plays pruriently upon the utopian longings of people by offering and selling set images intimating that special chosen celebrities and elite groups are destined to rule and administer just social codes that will make people happy and keep them in their proper places. Nothing is gray in the colored films of Disney, but the color camouflages the black-and-white view of good and evil in the world" (Zipes 2011: 26).

[25] "Our contemporary concept and image of a fairy tale has been shaped and standardized by Disney so efficiently through the mechanisms of the culture industry that our notions of happiness and utopia are and continue to be filtered through a Disney lens even if it is myopic" (Zipes 2011: 17).

> representations reproduce conservative stereotypes and carefully elude disruptions of patriarchal and heteronormative rules. (Wang 2025: 34, 47)

Consequently, there is still much to be done. The good news is that we are beginning to move toward what Jack Zipes (2011: 26) called a few years ago "De-disneyfication." All these translations are the beginning of new interpretations in which all the colors of Haroun's Sea of Stories come to light through the creation of new originals:

> and hence as the rewriting *and* creation of a new "original" in another language. Recognizing the indeterminacy of literary texts on the one hand, and the impossibility of "faithful" translation on the other, liberates the translator from servitude to the source from which the translation derives and undermines the old Romantic concept of authorship and at the same time revises simplistic notions of intentionality. (Bassnett 2014a: 153)

In all these cases, translation is not an act of preservation (of a definitive text), Scott argues, nor is it an act of recall (of a text that inevitably belongs to the past), "but an act of transmission (of handing on a text in what is deemed an appropriate form) and of reimagination ... Translation itself is constantly redrawing maps, redisposing the territories of language and cultures ... Translation does not merely register that change, that change's inevitability, but actively works to produce it" (Scott in Bassnett and Bush 2006: 109, 116).

5 Women's Translations of Men's Literature

Many women writers have dedicated works to rewriting stories told by male writers in literature. Thus, rewriting his-stories into herstories avoids the danger of a single story, for example in Yedda Morrison's *Darkness*, where she erasures and thus rewrites the first chapter of Joseph Conrad's *Heart of Darkness*, unmaking its colonialist, gendered discourse.

Another well-known case is Kathy Acker's novels. She states that "by repeating the past I transform it ... I try to destroy every law, every limitation." In her feminist punk rereading of *Don Quixote*, Don Quixote[26] is a woman and

---

[26] Of course, there are many other writers who have rewritten *Don Quijote* in some way or another. For instance, Shakespeare, Henry Fielding, Charles Dickens, Nikolai Gogol, Alphonse Daudet, Mark Twain, Gustave Flaubert, Benito Pérez Galdós, Chesterton or Graham Greene, among others, come to mind. And also in the arts, dance, opera, and so on, Salman Rushdie's *Quichotte* (2019) could be mentioned here as a translation of Cervantes in the Age of Anything-Can-Happen. Quichotte travels through time and space, In Rushdie's translation we find Hans Christian Andersen, the Beatles, Chaucer, Shakespeare, J. K. Rowling, El Greco, Giacometti, John Wayne, Humphrey Bogart, *Back to the Future, Men in Black,* Heidi Klum, *Candy Crush,* Elon Musk and Marcel Duchamp as the unsuccessful writer Sam DuChamp. Rushdie's Don Quijote does not live in La Mancha but in contemporary United States, perhaps that is why the novel does not begin with Cervantes's well-known sentence but with one typical of children's

all the other elements are also translated from a feminist perspective. Still another example is her novel *The Adult Life of Toulouse Lautrec*, in which Lautrec is actually a woman who narrates the life of her brother, Vincent van Gogh, while the prostitute Giannina describes the erotic memories of her experiences with the poet Ron Silliman. Acker also did a rewrite of *Great Expectations*. The story in novels like those by Kathy Acker questions convention and originality. Her relationship with the past is ironic, but at the same time it is intimately linked to what she wishes to undermine. These novels are rewritings of the past. They are translations of stories that are updated by transposing them into a more modern context. Because each text is many texts, as observed by Julia Kristeva, each word is an intersection of word, and each text is an absorption and transformation.

5.1 Jen Bervin's Sonnets

William Shakespeare is a canonical author who has been rewritten by many contemporary writers and artists.[27] Feminist criticism has scrutinized representations of gender in Shakespeare.[28] The Bard is revisited by Toni Morrison's

---

tales. The name of this translated *Quijote* is Ismail Smile. Ismail does not get mad reading romances but watching TV series and reality shows:

> There once lived, at a series of temporary addresses across the United States of America, a travelling man of Indian origin, advancing years and retreating mental powers, who, on account of his love for mindless television, had spent far too much of his life in the yellow light of tawdry motel rooms watching an excess of it, and had suffered a peculiar form of brain damage as a result. He devoured morning shows, daytime shows, late-night talk shows, soaps, situation comedies, Lifetime Movies, hospital dramas, police series, vampire and zombie serials, the dramas of housewives from Atlanta, New Jersey, Beverly Hills and New York, the romances and quarrels of hotel-fortune princesses and self-styled shahs, the cavortings of individuals made famous by happy nudities, the fifteen minutes of fame accorded to young persons with large social media followings on account of their plastic-surgery acquisition of a third breast or their post-rib-removal figures that mimicked the impossible shape of the Mattel company's Barbie doll, or even, more simply, their ability to catch giant carp in picturesque settings while wearing only the tiniest of string bikinis; as well as singing competitions, cooking competitions, competitions for business propositions, competitions for business apprenticeships, competitions between remote-controlled monster vehicles, fashion competitions, competitions for the affections of both bachelors and bachelorettes, baseball games, basketball games, football games, wrestling bouts, kickboxing bouts, extreme sports programming and, of course, beauty contests. (Rushdie 2019: 3–4)

[27] Supreme Court Justice Ruth Bader Ginsburg presiding over a mock appeal of the city's most notorious resident, Shylock, in a panel discussion of Shakespeare's *The Merchant of Venice* in 2017 comes to mind here.

[28] "Marianne Novy's *Women's Revisions of Shakespeare* (1990) explored how nineteenth-century authors including Charlotte Bronte, Emily Dickinson, and George Eliot incorporated and rewrote Shakespeare in their poetry and fiction; Novy's *Transforming Shakespeare:*

Desdemona (2011), Jeanette Winterson's *The Gap of Time* (2015), or Margaret Atwood's *Hag-Seed* (2016), to quote but a few. It has been translated by Steve McCaffery in his *Dark Ladies* (2016), by Gary Barwin in *Servants of Dust* (2015), or by Gregory Betts in *The Others Raisd in Me* (2009), among many others (see William Shakespeare's entry in Kostelanetz 2019). There are post-colonial feminist rewritings of Shakespeare's female characters, for example Sycorax and Miranda. In fact, many women writers talk back to Shakespeare (Carney 2022). I would like to focus here, however briefly, on Jen Bervin's translations of Shakespeare.

In many of her art projects, artist books and other works, Bervin plays with materiality. In *Nets* (2004/2019) she translates Shakespeare's *Sonnets*. We read both Bervin's poem in bold type and Shakespeare's in grey. It is a literal graphic palimpsest.[29] Bervin erases Shakespeare's sonnets playing with the blank of the page and with the font color of some words – those of the source text are faded and from them Bervin's poem emerges:

> I stripped Shakespeare's sonnets bare to the "nets" to make the space of the poems open, porous, possible -a divergent elsewhere. When we write poems, the history of poetry is with is, preinscribed in the white of the page; when we read or write poems, we do it with or against this palimpsest. (Bervin 2004/2019: n.p.)

Bervin erasures Shakespeare's sonnets to rewrite new (her)stories "printing sixty of his poems in a light gray font with a few scattered words printed in bold – generating or uncovering a second set of poems within Shakespeare's" (Altman 2021: n.p.). The original text remains recessive, floating faintly on the

---

Contemporary Women's Revisions in Literature and Performance (2000) and Julie Sanders's *Novel Shakespeares* (2001) turned to twentieth-century revisions by women writers such as Kate Atkinson, Angela Carter, Rita Dove, Gloria Naylor, Jane Smiley, and Marina Warner. Along with Novy and Sanders, the work of scholars Christy Desmet, Peter Erickson, Daniel Fischlin, Andrew Hartley, Alexa Huang, Sujata Iyengar, Margaret Jane Kidnie, Gordon McMullan, Elizabeth Rivlin, Ayanna Thompson, and many others, demonstrates that the creative and scholarly work of women 'talking back to Shakespeare' has continued to evolve along productive parallel lines" (Carney 2022: 1–2).

[29] "Here Jen Bervin's new text consists in a selection of a few words on another text. Whereas in a quotation, one borrows a prior text, one cuts one's from material from an older text and leaves the rest of the old text behind, here the new text seems to appear as a quotation within the older material, which the reader can apprehend fully. The layout of the old and the new texts seems to suggest that the new highlighted text in bold type is a foreign body in the density of the older text. While the new text is being traced over the surface of the older text, it doesn't rub it out. The new text becomes a synecdoche of the old one as well as its tangible ghost. This is once again a new literalisation of intertextuality: the eerie phenomenon of a to-and-fro movement between Shakespeare's and the new text experienced with the two other poems commented on above is made apparent on the page itself of Bervin's minimal production. So much so that it is almost impossible for the eyes to focus and adjust between grey and bold, thus creating a perpetual ongoing reading whose echoes are almost already traced" (Broqua 2010: 37–38).

page, but Bervin translates that history into a herstory by lifting some of the words out in darker ink, thus reimagining the original. She plays with the language, with the visual, with the materiality of words, and with the page seen as a canvas. Her text is "present-absent" (Bervin 2004/2019: 45), "vanishing or vanished" (Bervin 2004/2019: 63), "anchored" (Bervin 2004/2019: 137) in Shakespeare's text.

The result is a feminist in-between space which translates old histories in order to overcome the danger of a single story. That is why Bervin does not like the term "erasure," because her translations do not search loss but multiplicity. Bervin insists that what she tries to create are poems that point to the fact that many voices can be present:

> Her erasure not only unearths disparate meanings in but imagines alternative possibilities for Shakespeare's sonnets, cultivating new pleasures and beauties therein. Doing so, *Nets* begins to reveal how erasure can function as a powerful poetic mode for those whose subjectivities and voices have long been excluded from official literary and cultural histories: how erasure becomes a bold act of will. (Gold 2019: 89)

The very title, *Nets*, shows this process of intermingling of voices, of historical moments, of times, between two texts and two authors. Sonnets become Son**nets**. "Nets" is part of, is contained, in the previous title, *The Sonnets of William Shakespeare*:

> The title page of Bervin's edition, with its strong genitive, affirms Shakespeare's continued presence in the sequence that bears his name. Yet the "OF" that cements his ownership is printed in gray: Shakespeare's authority has fallen into shadow. Shakespeare, the title page suggests, both is and is not the author of this edition of his poems. How then does one cite this text? Who, exactly, is its author – Shakespeare or Bervin? Both? (Altman 2022: 490)

Bervin describes her process as making a whole with pieces missing. These missing pieces, the cracks and fissures left bare are the most remarkable parts of her work; these, she says, are the places where things happen:

> This sense of bibliographic hesitation deepens when one opens the volume. Bervin reproduces sixty sonnets in light but legible gray text. In each, she prints a handful of words in a bold, black typeface, forming a second set of poems within Shakespeare's. Fragmentary, epigrammatic, Bervin's poems emerge from the *Sonnets* without fully distinguishing themselves from it, or fully erasing it. (Altman 2022: 490)

Nets subverts historical boundaries and the historical distance between both authors, or between author and "translator." Bervin offers a creative translation in Scott's sense (Scott 2009), a translation that is a process rather than a product. This process brings into being of "the potentialities of the source text, in and through (a version) of the target text" (Wilson and Gerber 2012: ix). Her *Nets* survives because of its capacity "to ramify and diversify, intralingually, interlingually and intersemiotically" (Scott 2009: 39).

Bervin's translations – not only *Nets* but also textile translations such as *The Desert* (2008) or *The Dickinson Composites* (2004–2008) – offer creative translations that are not static but show us how the canon "might be expanded to accommodate new voices and textual forms, creating space for continual reinventions in our understanding of subjectivity and verse" (Gold 2019: 104). *Nets* could be described as an adventure in readerly consciousness and an experience of language. Translation is seen here not as a test of comprehension but "of the fruitfulness of our inability to comprehend ... Translation must be allowed to open up and develop its own multimedial discursive space. It ceases to be a discipline ('translation studies') and becomes a philosophical enquiry into its own functions and possible relationships with the translator's being-in-the-world" (Scott in Campbell and Vidal 2019: 88). The result is "a poetics of temporal fracture, which both disrupts linear time and participates in it" (Altman 2022: 492).

Nets is a feminist translation where the male pronouns are moved "into the gray text. In Bervin's black text, men are not addressed" (Altman 2022: 497).[30] Bervin's translation of Shakespeare's Son**nets** is a trace (inter)woven with traces:

> Translation is a trace: of what was there before, of what I was before. It is also engraved, woven through with traces: of our individual and collective past, of our histories and our stories, of our memories and of the tales we tell about who we were and how we came to be who we are. This has important consequences for the social and historical functions of translation. (Polezzi 2020: 338)

Bervin calls into question the authoritative original "with recognition of the history of unequal power relations between languages and cultures ... Today, translation seems to be everywhere, and there is a sense that perhaps, at last, Western literary scholarship is starting to acknowledge the role played by translation in the movement of literatures through time and space" (Bassnett 2014b: 55). Bassnett goes on to say that translation is essential to the interrelationship between literatures, "to the continuation of literary traditions and to the introduction of the new, the foreign, the different. Significantly, more writers

---

[30] It has also been analyzed as a text of queer resistance (Gold 2019).

than ever before have started to use translation metaphorically" (Bassnett 2014b: 56). Jen Bervin is one of those writers.

5.2 Telling Tales with Patience Agbabi's Chaucer

Another case of a canonical male writer who has been translated by contemporary female authors is Geoffrey Chaucer. The feminist translation of Chaucer is a clear example of the original premise of this Element, as suggested earlier, for instance, by Alonzi (2023a, 2024), when he described translation as an act of synchronization, disrupting and resetting time, and the task of the historian and that of the translator as creative acts which give new life to a text. This is instantiated particularly in his Alison from *The Canterbury Tales*. Alison of Bath has had a dramatic impact across time, perhaps because she is

> the first ordinary woman in English literature ... the first mercantile, working, sexually active woman – not a virginal princess or queen, not a nun, witch, or sorceress, not a damsel in distress nor a functional servant character, not an allegory. A much-married woman and widow, who works in the cloth trade and tells us about her friends, her tricks, her experience of domestic abuse, her long career combatting misogyny, her reflections on the ageing process, and her enjoyment of sex, Alison exudes vitality, wit, and rebellious self-confidence. Alison is a character whom readers across the centuries have usually seen as accessible, familiar, and, in a strange way, real. For many people she is by far the most memorable of the Canterbury pilgrims. (Turner 2023: 2)

Alison is ordinary and at the same time she is extraordinary. She is a mosaic of many misogynist voices she confronts. She is a woman who "tells jokes, enjoys sex, and thinks for herself about the male canon and the exclusion of women's voices full of wit," and who uses her rhetorical technique and personal experience to go "head-to-head with the most authoritative of authorities" (Turner 2023: 3). There are many readings of Alison. Dryden and Pope tried to make her less scandalous. Voltaire also took her on. Across the Atlantic she went on the stage. The twentieth century read her from a communist perspective. Ted Hughes also referred to her. And many others (Turner 2023).

In the twenty-first century, there are many rewritings of Alison. Some of the most interesting ones are those translations in which "Alison reinvented herself through new authors in postcolonial Britain. Over the last couple of decades we have seen Black female poets voicing, performing, rewriting, and rethinking Alison" (Turner 2023: 227). For instance, Karen King-Aribisala's *Kicking Tongues* (1988), Gloria Naylor's *Bailey's Café* (1992), Jean "Binta" Breeze's *The Wife of Bath Speaks in Brixton Market* (2000), Marilyn Nelson's *Cachoeira Tales* (2005), or Zadie Smith's *The Wife of Willesden* (2022), among many others. In these cases, Alison becomes a black woman "with a transnational identity that stretches across multiple cultures. In each version, she is written by a woman – finally, women have decisively started to claim Alison's voice after hundreds of years of male appropriations" (Turner 2023: 227–228). Although each of these works is extremely relevant and groundbreaking, I would like to concentrate here first on Patience Agbabi's *Telling Tales* (2014) and the on Caroline Bergvall's *Alisoun* (2019).

Agbabi's *Telling Tales* is the transcription of a poetry slam that takes place on a Routemaster bus travelling from London to Canterbury, where the pilgrims compete to see who can produce the best tale on their way to Becket's tomb. Agbabi was fascinated by the Wife of Bath. So, she wrote first "The Wife of Bafa" (2000): a composite of The Wife of Bath in the *Prologue*, the exuberant Prologue to her Tale; and Mrs X. "The Wife of Bafa" (2000) was a rewriting of the Wife of Bath's Prologue, in Nigerian English. It was published in the collection *Transformatrix*. In 2014, she published *Telling Tales*, a remix of the entire text, including every single tale. In this remixing,

> it was my duty to add the tale of the Loathly Lady. I must remix my own remix. And in doing this, I had to *enrich* my original. By adding the tale, the Wife of Bafa became a more complex character, the shadow of the big man soldier's rape permeating the story which is far more problematic for a contemporary audience as he seems to be rewarded rather than punished for his crime. He gets the girl and they all live happily ever after! My Wife could not help but comment on this: "So she married a rapist/but he learnt his lesson. / May God give us young submissive husband!" In true storytelling fashion, I echoed the character and narrative structure of the original but added phrases and detail peculiar to my own creation. (Agbabi 2018: 3)

Agbabi argues that anticolonial politics can also be found in texts that elect, as hers does, to retain Chaucer's London setting, "since the former colonial headquarters has changed profoundly to become the multicultural metropolis it is today" (D'Arcens 2021: 13). Thus, she rewrites Chaucer for the twenty-first century. Chaucer's pilgrims varied in gender, social rank, age, geographical origin, and occupations. Agbabi's pilgrimage is a contemporary multiracial and multiethnic cast of storytellers:

> I redressed the pilgrim's gender balance to a 50:50 split; settings were altered – tales take place in every part of the UK plus Nigeria, Ghana, Denmark, and Russia. And it was imperative the pilgrims came from, that is originated from, "every shires ende/Of Engelond" and beyond: Scotland, Wales, Northern Ireland, France, Germany, India, Nigeria, Zimbabwe, Canada, St Lucia. A multicultural motley crew. I wanted to reflect the demographics of contemporary Britain via Chaucer's poetics. (Agbabi 2018: 2)

"The Wife of Bafa" is expanded in this text "to include a version of the tale set in Ghana, as well as the prologue" (Turner 2023: 231). Agbabi broadens the reach of the tale to the next English-speaking country west of Nigeria, Ghana:

> It was important that the tale was from somewhere else: the cultural truth of Ghana's matrilineal society – "the female owns the children not de male" fits well with the power of the queen to potentially kill the rapist knight. My wife is based in London and Lagos – like Chaucer's original, she is well travelled. She is constantly crossing boundaries, referring to "this London" and "Victoria Island," the most exclusive district in Lagos. Though she is now married to the Nigerian "Bafa," previous husbands came from other countries: "the first from Ghana, second Sierra Leone, / the third was white Englishman." She buys and sells cloth "lace, linen, and Dutch wax." Again, there is significance that the popular prints that are associated with West Africa originate from The Netherlands (it was as close to Ypres, Belgium, as I could get). To remain in character, she later refers to "Kente cloth/traditional dress of Ghana."
> This Nigerian Wife of Bath, partially educated and self-sufficient, is a woman of the world. (Agbabi 2018: 4)

That is why Agbabi tells the tale in *Nigerian* English; not Nigerian Pidgin, Broken English "that would not reflect the fact that she was well-travelled and used to addressing Western audiences; and not Standard English that would have placed her in a very different social class. Nigerian English represented her cross-culturality" (Agbabi 2018: 4). Agbabi's language represents the context of a multicultural, postcolonial London. Thus, Agbabi performs an effective critique of the colonizer's linguistic norm. Her Wife of Bath, Alice Bafa, is a businesswoman whose monologue

> is performed in a marked Nigerian accent. Agbabi did not grow up in a Nigerian English environment and she performs predominantly in Standard English. She has thus worked on her English, vivifying it with Nigerian structures and rhythms in order to convey the different experiences now inhabiting Chaucer's tradition; as the poet has argued, "by 'translating' Middle English into Nigerian English, [she] hoped to retain an earthiness and an otherness, that standard English would tame" (Agbabi 2015). In keeping with this, Agbabi abandons Chaucer's rhyming couplets and transforms the presentation of her character as it exists in the General Prologue into a monologue. (Coppola 2015: 8)

Agbabi shows that feminist translations are "not the repetition of a text in another language, but a complicity between texts to converge on something that lies beyond them" (Scott 2018: 31). Chaucer's third-person description the Wife is here replaced "by a bold and proud first-person presentation of the Nigerian businesswoman" (Coppola 2015: 8), showing contemporary interconnections between postcolonial theory and medievalism:

> My name is Mrs Alice Ebi Bafa
> I come from Nigeria.
> I am very fine, isn't it?
> My next birthday I'll be ... twenty-nine.
> I'm business woman. (Agbabi 2014: 31)

Mrs. Alice Ebi Bafa is a businesswoman in a global world. She sells cloth, "I've all de latest styles from Lagos" and also "Italian shoe an' handbag to match, / lace, linen an' Dutch wax" (Agbabi 2014: 31).

As in the case of Jen Bervin, in my opinion Agbabi's translation of Chaucer can be seen as a trace, but also as co-presence, which has political and ethical consequences:

> Translation – translation as trace, as co-presence, as the negotiation and renegotiation, the mediation and remediation of sameness and diversity – is at the core of that ethics, at the core of our ability to recognize ourselves through the thread of change, to see ourselves in others and others in ourselves, and to acknowledge that home is always made on the move but also that someone can always remove our homes from us. An ethics of translation as co-presence allows us to remain hospitable and to recognize the reciprocity always inscribed in hospitality, without exacting the price of erasure or imposing it upon ourselves. (Polezzi 2020: 340)

Patience Agbabi compels us to think about translation as a collaboration, as a relationship between two people, "one of whom wrote a text in one time and place, another who encountered that text and reconfigured it anew somewhere else. It also raises the basic question ... what exactly is the relationship between a so-called original and a so-called translation?" (Bassnett 2014b: 57).

5.3 Rewriting Chaucer with Caroline Bergvall's Alisoun

Many of Caroline Bergvall's artworks stem from the idea that revisionist narratives are crucial for any shift to happen and for any other vision to take root. Her work is based on that premise: that to bring about the end of this particularly lethal form of identitarian hold, and patriarchal structuring, "one needs to break through it, at its words, in its myths and depths, in its laws and archetypes and social structures. In this sense they lead and support other revolutionary moves" (personal communication).

Her work is definitely part of this. Some of her literary works also take Chaucer as her starting point. In fact her Chaucer inspired texts "The Franker Tale" or "The Fried Tale" are two very strong and angry tales that in a way precede and accompany *Alisoun*. It is precisely on *Alisoun* that I would like to focus. Caroline Bergvall's *Alisoun Sings* (2019), committed to the wife of Bath, the proto-feminist wife of Bath in Chaucer's *Canterbury Tales* that fascinates Agbabi, is a particularly interesting feminist translation of the *Canterbury Tales*. Alisoun is an exploded "she," or "her." More than "she," elsewhere than "she." More than gender. Bergvall's Alisoun is not within the bounds that gender and its essentialized archetypes wants to allocate. "She is she-they-he-we-I!" (personal communication). Alisoun represents a "her" that, according to Bergvall, needs to be broadened, to shape great pluri-gender, cross-gender archetypes.

Bergvall changes the name of Chaucer's Alison, so that it does not "son," taking the reader away from any patriarchal interpretation and playing with "soun" or "soon":

> The name *Alisoun* contains a typically rich Bergvallian pun: she is not a "son" but a "soun" – a "soon." She is askew, out of joint from the typical progress of patrilineal descent. She is *soonness* itself – a prospect, a future. If the book begins with a pun, it thus also begins with a paradox: the future, Bergvall suggests, resides in the past. (Altman 2020: n.p.)

In the same line, at the end of *Alisoun Sings* we read "Hystoricise!" (Bergvall 2019: 191), a translation of Fredric Jameson's well-known "Always historicize." Bergvall changes the typography and thus avoids the word "*his*tory" in favor of all stories:

> Bergvall's Middle English spelling of this paradigmatically modern word *sounds* the same as Jameson's "historicize." However, the inaudible shift from *i* to *y* announces a commensurate shift in historical practice: a refusal of *his*toricism in favor of an anachronistic, queer, and anti-disciplinary engagement with the past. The shift in spelling also activates dormant semantic associations that haunt the standard spelling. *Hy*storicise calls to mind, for instance, *hy*steria, that 19th century disease of patriarchy – implying that historicism itself is a patriarchal discipline, an expression of a controlling heterotemporality. (Altman 2020: n.p.)

As a translation of Chaucer's Wife Alisoun resonates as a cluster of sounds, as a provocative voice that calls up other voices. In her trilogy, *Meddle English* (2011), *Drift* (2014) and *Alisoun Sings* (2019) she translates the past through the signified and the signifier. There are not only words in English, French, and Middle English, but also typographic and sonic mixtures of languages and rewritings of the content of History into herstories. It all started with *Shorter*

Chaucer Tales (2006), a sequence of five poems commissioned by Charles Bernstein and David Wallace in 2006 for the biennial congress of the New Chaucer Society. These *Tales*, written in a dystopic and transhistoric English, are published in her *Meddle English* (2011). These stories are the beginning of a cycle in which she creates some of the translation games used for her historical texts.

The catalog titled *Middling English* (2010), from the installation of the same name, is also very thought-provoking. That catalogue, now out of print, shows the broadsides[31] she created for some of the Chaucer pieces prior to *Alisoun Sings* (2019). This catalog begins with an epigraph from Glissant's *Poetics of Relation*: "We no longer reveal totality within ourselves by lightning flashes. We approach it through the accumulation of sediments" (in Bergvall 2010: n.p.). This is undoubtedly the basis for the subsequent presentation by Bergvall (2010: 9), where she explains how this accumulation of sediments will develop:

> For this Project, I want to create active circuits, a circulation between historical elements and contemporary narratives. A circulatory structure of writings, sounds, and objects. An installed trajectory, a spatial platform of different elements, and different materials, manifested through some central methodological concerns: the site as working structure – language as primary material – writing as mode of hand-to-hand exchange and pleasure – historical research around the development of the English language – listening stations – abstract poetic theatre.

Bergvall goes on to say that the space she is going to create is a political, subversive, messy, rhizomatic, deterritorialized, opaque, in-process, open space, where everything is interrelated, with "lines that draw from one node to another" (Bergvall 2010: 10). This is her translating space:

> I will create a space that is both sparse and satirical, messy and structural, which addresses processes of interconnection, intercalation, distribution, interception – what it means, positively, to be tied to everything else – especially as societal accelerations around the criminalization of citizens and residents, the suspicion of the foreigner, the well-rigged immunity of corporate corruption, are disempowering and disabling: imagination must rip rule again! (Bergvall 2010: 9)

As in previous cases, Bergvall sees translation as a recreation, as a political way to reinvent the past, as an interaction with other texts that does not have a resting point. In *Alisoun Sings* we find a character called Caroline who tells Alisoun she is "bringing me back to my own time, slowly more grounded and available, full of a fighting spirit … a necessary traumatised transition that

---

[31] https://carolinebergvall.com/work/broadsides/.

rekindles reconnections, as much as tough, persistent cooperation" (Bergvall 2019: 58).

While Chaucer's three women do not interact with each other, Bergvall's Alisouns form a network in which they tell stories. In *Alisoun Sings*, among others, Bergvall demonstrates that it is possible to create translations by

> using a process of translation as a way to reinvent or recreate the final word so that by explicating different spellings, different words for the same words, or through homophonic translation, there's historical depth. It opens up the semantic field. It's a way of writing.
>
> In *Alisoun* you find it also in the pronouns, with "het, hem, em," which allows us to rethink what is actually being said: Is it a pronoun? Is it a verb? That kind of play on the pronoun is similarly translated. Rather than having a translator go from A to B, it becomes an AB-type thing. Translation doesn't have a resting point neither here nor there. But it spans that stretch. It comes across so many interactions. There's no final mastery in translation because it's taken over by the performative one way or another (Bergvall in Nissan 2019: n.p.).

Alisoun Sings is the closing volume of this feminist trilogy comprising *Meddle English* (2011) and *Drift* (2014). The work on Alisoun, a contemporary translation of Chaucer's Wife of Bath, started with Bergvall's ongoing need, previously explored in "The Franker Tale" and "The Fried Tale," to plunge into a strong narrative process of voicing and voices. It first came out in 2008 as *Alyson Singes* in a limited edition of seventy-five copies published by Belladonna, now out of print. *Alyson Singes* remains "the structural 'spine'" of what became *Alisoun Sings* nearly ten years later.

In the book she wanted to emphasize further "the multiplicity of voices and the heteroglossia of lived embedded gendered/sexualised/racialised voices/lives and multiple narratives" (Bergvall, personal communication). The book also preexisted in a few pieces from *Middling English* including "1DJ2MANY" (a live soundwork as well as a recording and installation[32]), the call "O SIS" (a broadside, a live work, and also an installed sound piece[33]), and the soundwork "Pink Trombone," written for and during the global Women's March of January 2017 and partly reproduced in the book. It was commissioned and played on Internet radio in eight different countries as part of Documenta14 (Kassel &Athens).

---

[32] https://carolinebergvall.com/work/1dj2many-installed/.
[33] https://soundcloud.com/carolinebergvall/osis?utm_source=clipboard&utm_medium=text&utm_campaign=social_sharing.

Charles Bernstein[34] highlights Bergvall's approach to this work as an acoustic performance: "*Alyson Singes* overlays Chaucerian sound patterning onto contemporary sites; a dazzling, politically charged realization of diachronic vernacular, the old emerging from the new like mist from a deep fissure." In effect, *Alisoun Sings* explodes Chaucer's "The Wife of Bath's Tale" using the voice of Alisoun, who is a composite of many contemporary women artists, activists, and writers, from Emma Goldman to Audre Lorde, Pussy Riot, or Vivienne Westwood, among many others. *Alisoun Sings* is a palimpsest in which the reader finds quotations by Nina Simone, Patti Smith, Hannah Arendt, Hélène Cixous, Arundhati Roy, Nancy Spero, Mona Hatoum, Virginia Woolf, and Kathy Acker, disco songs, Internet slang, and a reference to the 2017 Women's March, among others. In "1DJ2MANY," Alisoun offers a pastiche of present and past voices, of contemporary song lyrics related to sex, and in "Herte" she herself appears as the "author."

Alisoun is a shaker. She uses homophones, false friends, and an unruly language which looks for resonances. Alisoun gives voice to many silenced voices, from the *Me Too* movement to *Black Lives Matter*. She is a collectivist voice "yet made up of individual and individualist moments, practitioners, poets, writers, both old and new. I was not making a claim for her as a collective, but she is made of so many explicit bits and voices, that such a voicing is a claim of a memory structure that belongs to many, for lack of better word" (Bergvall in Nissan 2019: n.p.). Language here is heteroglossic, polyvocal, and collectivist. Thus, in "Copyist" we read the following:

> Do allocate someone to copy exchanges in your partee or you'll find that ne can make heads nor tales of whatswhat after awhile can lead all kinds of misreadings & typos oons th' ink has dried. And what with inattention, coffee stains, drippings and the likes, unfortunates pellings get tuff to hiden or changen, like bad tatts covering bad tatts, as chaucer the aufeur famously bemoaned. (Bergvall 2019: 3)

This is a clear example of the idea that translations "are original while embodying aspects of copying ... all creative works do, ... translations as nothing but copies founder on both linguistic and philosophical grounds" (Malmkjær 2020: 4).

For Bergvall, quoting is a recognition, a way to acknowledge influences from many different cultural backgrounds, "carrying in ones body the burden of otheres pain." As she argues in "Spero,"

---

[34] www.audiaturbok.no/forlag/belladonna-books/alyson-singes.

> Right on! xlaims what artist Nancy Spero, I've copied out reports hung them on the gallery walls for all to see the terror and the torture, rape by numbers, rape by camps, sometimes copying typing out stamping quoting taking on, still making work out of clean-ups like a Ligon, like a Lacy, carrying in ones body the burden of otheres pain, otheres codex skin as ones work, kepen each truthe each testament alive, relived individually recorporated testified & geloved like a Piper a Hiller a Boltanski, docu leaking body leaking holding on to proof & dataflow in an age that chastises, isolates what it debases, turns into mass what it depersonalizes. (Bergvall 2019: 43)

Bergvall's Alisoun tells "*her*" stories," not "History," in an "upfolded over updoubled" language (Bergvall 2019: 3), rewriting form and content:

> Hi you all, I'm Alisoun. Some people call me Al. Am many things to many a few thyinge to some & nothing but an irritant to socialites and othere glossing troglodytes. I dig a good chat banter aboute. Sbeen a long time, some & six hundred times have circled round the solar sun, everything were different yet pretty much the same, sunsets were reddier, godabov ruled all & the franks the rest. Womenfolk were owned trafeckt regulated petted tightlye impossible to run ones own afferes let alone ones mynd nat publicly nat privatly, & so were most workfolk enserfed, owned never free, working working day 'n niht. Sunsets redder, legs a little shorter. (Bergvall 2019: 1)

Alisoun articulates an alternate vision, one in which the institutions of patriarchal life and the genders it constructs to enforce those institutions are changeable and changing:

> ... I like to think I move with the times. As agenders change and the oceans rise and the citees sprawl, mariage needs be large! accountable! not reserved for the benefits of one, needs revise its views on ownership & burghery. (Altman 2020: n.p.)

Bergvall plays with the word "Burghery," which includes "burgher" and "buggery." Her language is weirdo, rude, since she is speechin many langages at once:

> Btw nat worry should ma language feeling it weirdo, rude_& cueryous at fi rst. Rough as a cats lick or like a dress whats travagant, folded over updoubled, as though am speechin many langages at once. Whats foshur! And many stories too! In many gay apparel! Picture me standing on each side of the silver cli_ s of Cinque_& Caletum like standing at Midlina across the silfra crack, am astride he world joining two moats, the northern sea rushing between my herculean legs splashes against the mixed wools of my quim. No but for serious, 'tis a rich scrambljumbl of heavily crossbedded bitching tongues, folded like shells in tymologick tension, so is ma usage a happy combimess, simple. (Bergvall 2019: 3–4)

Language "both connecks and divides" (Bergvall 2019: 4). Language and its ability to tell stories is a network. The same is true for translation, which is not a linear process but rather an entangled, relational one that excavates and brings to light new connections. What matters is the capacity to create networks, links, and resonances:

> It starts with a name. We pronounce her name. It rings across the room and disappears down the corridors of time. It disperses across spaces, travels through folded mineral lives, and comes to rest softly, a heartbeat waiting to be picked up. It matters little at this stage where the name comes from and whether it belongs to a historical, a mythical or a literary figure. What matters is the network of resonance that it brings up. What matters is its capacity to pull up events, sceneries, struggles as well as crowds of contradictory, marvellous, spirited beings in its sonorous wake. We call her name. She hears us calling. It rings out from many cycles, past and future set in motion. A voice starts to speak. (Bergvall 2019: vii)

Perhaps that is why in one of her interviews, Bergvall states (Nissan 2019: n. p.): "I consider *Alisoun Sings* to be translative in spirit." It is no coincidence that in that same Preface, she continues to say:

> Tales lead to more tales. Stories get woven from multitudes of stories. Voices call up other voices. A voice is a voice-cluster. I sense her coming through as a concert of sounds and lives and purposes from a vast patchwork of influences, events, and emotions that accord with her, and revitalise her presence among us. Her persona, her phrasing, her intentions, her clothes, her geographies, emerge, available, recyclable and drawn out from the infinite details and impulses of a great range of cultural, personal, physical even psychological reaches and attractions. (Bergvall 2019: viii)

The stories already told must be told in another way. Stories are rewritten with the multitude of voices that have been silenced until now:

> And no future achademye can ever change fact that ma tongue is as agile with it as a french kiss or a sailing cog in the storm. Anyways when comes to speeching and telling, no need for perfeck, nor for clevrest. Whoever needed sore long words anyways, like that giant protein made up of 189,819 letters what takes 4 hours to pronounce? Ive gotta traders grammar, lovers declension, indeedy me loins may stoppe blede, will get to that, but ma lovejuice is out of this worlde, has just begun aflowe the banks and whan I speech like this ma thoughts & aventures, tis like I am ysitting the lap of Sherazade & she axe for it 2 be longe 2 be loude, thats my whole megafony! Minde yow these dayes ofen wishe ma weight of talent can prophesise like a Cassandra, provoke uprisings liche Bouddicca and runne molten lava all over this Trompeii!! I hope whats clarified it? No foolery. Ma word's ma bond. Ma name's Alison, Dames Alison. (Bergvall 2019: 5)

It is necessary to translate the stories that those in power have already told. For this reason, these translations are actually original, since they offer stories, stories, which are no longer History but herstories. That is why for Bergvall, translation is a Benjaminian construction site, which is never finished and is constantly changing. She uses translation to reinvent and recreate. She is interested in the residual and political implications of the middles and margins (Owens 2015: 147–148). By rewriting and quoting previous voices, "Bergvall herself is acting as a sort of translator by simply recasting preexisting texts into a new poem that is entirely her own" (Goldsmith 2011: 194).

Through her performances but also in her books, whose pages are in many cases, canvases with words and letters in constant movement, Bergvall translates with what Coldiron (2012: 197, 198) calls "generative residues," which are "phonemes; retained foreign refrain lines; untranslated slang, dialogue, dialect or names; or allusions to foreign places and cultural practices." Although these residues may be immediately present in the text itself, in some cases, they "may be enhanced by the textual technology (as when printers place foreign words in a different typeface). Yet residues may variously serve as resistant, celebratory or subversive traces of alterity. In any case, they invite historically contextualized cultural analysis." Through her bodily translations, her voice makes us *feel* translation:

> A recording of Bergvall, for instance, reveals multilingual phonetic wordplay making unexpected meanings that could not exist without highly visible – which here means audible – alterity (Bergvall n.d.). It may take time to press visibility into as full a coordination with the present age's literary aesthetic as was the case in the medieval or early modern periods ... aesthetic efforts following artists like Mayer, Bernstein or Bergvall might well come to depend on the co-artist's – that is, the translator's – visibility. (Coldiron 2012: 197, 198)

The visibility to which Coldiron appeals, when referring to Bergvall, is the best summary of the contemporary need to listen to all voices, all stories. The urgency to achieve the "[r]ebirth of the songer, of the teller" (Bergvall 2010: 16).

5.4 Perverse Herstories: Erin Mouré's Transelations

The previous examples show how linear History, understood as a coherent whole, has evaporated, and the remaining stories are located on the margins of meaning and syntax, where the representation of what cannot be represented is a veritable maelstrom without a reference. In this section I will refer to Erin

Mouré's *trans*elations, for instance *Sheep's Vigil by a Fervent Person* (2001), which exemplify what Sherry Simon calls "perverse translations."

The multiple forms she has used to write her name reflects her search for multiplicity and mobility and for a porous and not rooted identity, always in connection with other bodies and with their surroundings. Since *O Cidadán* (2002), she has used most commonly Erín Moure; prior to that it was mostly Erin Mouré (Williams and Marinkova 2015: 74). *Sheep's Vigil by a Fervent Person* is written under the name Eirin Moure. She adds the *i* in homage to Alberto Caeiro, one of Pessoa's many heteronyms – she also uses heteronyms in *The Unmemntioable* (2012).[35] As Lily Robert-Foley (2024) argues, her own name, Erín Moure, could be considered a kind of heteronym. In this respect, it is also relevant to note that

> although she signs the book on the cover with accent shifted, the copyright page bears her father's surname, complicating the economic and symbolic registers of her gesture. Interestingly, this is the last time that "Mouré" appears on any of her copyright pages: from Little Theatres (2005) onward, both cover and copyright are signed Moure. Moreover, Moure seems to be making a pun by freighting "perdure" with its double, "perjure," in her opening questions, which I quote again, "can the name be reinvested or infested, fenestrated … set in motion again? Unmoored? Her semblance? Upsetting the structure/stricture even momentarily. (Maguire 2015: 53)

Douglas Robinson (2022: 141) considers the heteronymous translator as "profoundly subversive." No doubt, this is the case of Moure/Mouré. Heteronyms refer to a game in which the creation causes the creator to disappear. The author's presence stems from their absence. Both authorship and originality become blurred and diffuse. Mouré's heteronyms appear in her trans*e*lations, in spaces that are neither homogeneous nor unidirectional but contradictory and slippery. Heteronomy compels us to ask ourselves whether it is the writer who creates and constructs the texts or, conversely, whether it is the texts that create and construct the writer, particularly since the author's name is an unstable signifier that gives rise to multiple interpretations. Mouré (2009: 176) explains that Pessoa created multiple characters called heteronyms who wrote poetry because he insisted on the need of a plurality of the self in a plural

---

[35] "[*The Unmemntioable*] is produced by the interplay of two voices that cannot quite articulate their chosen subject. These are Moure's already familiar heteronyms: E. M. (Erín Moure), who visits Velyki Hlibovychi in Eastern Galicia (today Ukraine) to bury her mother's ashes, and E. S. (Elisa Sampedrín, from the other Galicia, of northwestern Spain), who is making an attempt at 'researching "experience"' in the Romanian capital Bucharest (*Unmemntioable* 37). While E. M. struggles with the task of writing about her grief for her mother and a distant landscape traumatized by ethnic and political strife, E.S. is unable to conceptualize experience that transcends and precedes language" (Williams and Marinkova 2015: 76).

universe. That is why Mouré trans*e*lation of Pessoa doesn't adhere "to a fluent notion of translation, but to an exorbitance. Exorbit happenstance. Exstance. Extantiation. A performative gesture altering space, altering the original, and altering my own voice and capacity in English. All of which is, I think, the best that translation can do" (Mouré 2009: 177).

In her trans*e*lation, Moure or Mouré translates *O guardador de rebanhos* (1914) by Alberto Caeiro, one of Fernando Pessoa's many heteronyms. Erin Mouré/Eirin Moure plays with Portuguese and English, adds lines, makes languages interact, locates Fernando Pessoa/Alberto Caeiro in a different scenario, and from the Portuguese countryside the "original" is translated to urban Toronto. Her trans*e*lation is a rewriting, a way of "generating texts in response to another text written in a different language" (Quéma 2021: 28). Although she departures significantly from the Portuguese texts, she insists that her work is a translation:

> I see this book as a translation, as faithful, even if different. That's why it appears in a bilingual edition with the Portuguese originals – my deflections of Pessoa's texts are thus *visible*, even if you do not read Portuguese. I want this book to be judged not just as my poetry but as translations of Pessoa. Trans-*e*-lations. Trans-eirin-elations. Transcreations. (Mouré 2001: ix)

Mouré and Moure rewrite(s) Pessoa and Caeiro in many ways.[36] Sherry Simon (2006: 152) argues that the fact Pessoa was "a writer of transformations . . . authorize Mouré to use Pessoa as a device of her own self-transformation." Mouré's are "degrees of translation," that is, "practices of language-crossing that remain incomplete, that defy the regulatory function of translation and result in mixed forms of expression. The claim on the other language is an element of creation, a mode of composition" (Simon 2006: 128). No doubt, she goes too far in her rewritings. Her translations are "irreverent" (Simon 2006: 151). But instead of seeing this as a negative trait (Braz 2009), Simon understands her trans*e*lations as transformations. She reshapes Pessoa and at the same time is reshaped by the writing process (Simon 2006: 151–152). Eirin Moure's rewriting of Alberto Caeiro is an excellent example of women's

---

[36] As the book description explains: "From the Portuguese countryside and roaming sheep of 1914, a 21st century Toronto emerged, its neighborhoods still echoing the 1950s, their dips and hollows, hordes of wild cats, paved creeks. Her poem became a translation, the jubilant and irrepressible vigil of a fervent person. 'Suddenly,' says Mouré impishly, 'I had found my master.' Caeiro's sheep were his thoughts and his thoughts, he claimed, were all sensations. Mouré's sheep are stray cats and from her place in Caeiro's poetry, she creates a woman alive in an urban world where the rural has not vanished, where the archaic suffuses us even when we do not beckon it, and yet the present tense floods us fully. In this ecstatic long poem of hope and creeks and cats and rain, Sheep's Vigil by a Fervent Person catches Governor General's Award-winner Erin Mouré at her most playful and ingenuous and wearing her Galician name."

(re)telling told stories for the first time. To read Moure is to read Caeiro with a different voice. It is the same story told *again for the first time* in a more playful way,

> using today's places and slangy words, today's references to Iraq and missiles, to Lake Ontario, and the Humber Valley, to Winnett Street, and Vaughan Road. But it is Pessoa's voice, his irony and gentle derision of the world. For Pessoa's sheep and countryside and suspicion of the piano, Mouré offers cats and Winnett Street and the manhole cover you can overcover and hear the creek run. Pessoa's pain is Mouré's "torn ankle," and the landscape of night becomes "Trinity-Bellwood up to Christie Pits and on to No Frills" … a wooden carriage becomes "my neighbour's old car, Roaring pointlessly every morning on Winnett"; "Ah to be a wooden carriage, says Pessoa, I wouldn't need hopes, only wheels" … "What I'd give to be the creek under the road at No Frills," says Mouré, when Pessoa speaks of a river and laundresses … Mouré calls into being the simultaneous existence of contrary things: the country in the city, Pessoa in Toronto, Portuguese in English. These equivalences are both true and untrue: they are historical traces that persist, hidden, into the present. (Simon 2006: 153–154)

In this regard, Moure (2021: 13) states that when we read, "we translate from one tongue into the 'same' tongue, though the same is never the same." This is relevant, since to her "reading is where thought risks" (Moure 2009: 13). Herself a translator – for instance of Nicole Brossard – she argues that some works like Elisa Sampedrín's *O Resplandor* confound notions of authorship and translation (Moure 2021: 8). The act of translating is for Moure an embodied and sensorial process:

> The body that reads and responds to light and from which language emerges, is the body of translation. When light hits the mouth in that resplandor of reading, time reverses, to the time of first writing, unoriginal but a point of origin, it emits another time, text, into the mouth and body of the reader … To translate is … [t]o allow language into your mouth, your circadian rhythm, which is to say, your existence. It is part of a continuum of transformations, of which the body is both subject and conduit … In such a space, how can we now describe what is a true translation, a faithful one? To what I seek in being in language, what is added when I open my mouth to the light of an/other language/s? What is it to be affected in your mouth by the passage of time and to have this passage alter time itself, and thus alter you. Via the work of another. This, necessarily. Through the work of another. (Moure 2021: 14, 15)

Every time we read a text, she says, we translate: "The job of the translator, her task or *aufgabe* (role, mandate, duty, remit, mission, responsibility) lies here, in this third space between artefact of language (book, text, screen) and receptor of language. To translate is not simply to read, it is the task or mission of the translator" (Mouré 2021: 14). That is why Moure chooses the "intranslatable," following Augusto de Campos's "intradução," instead of the "untranslatable" that appears in the first English version of Cassin's et al. *Dictionary of Untranslatables*. Moure argues that intranslatable implies that a translation is never finished. Translating is dynamic, performative, interrelated to other translations that came before (Grass 2023). Moure's "intranslatable" is, in Barthesian terms, embodied, "unreaderly": "it burns in the mouth. It alters the reading body, and the altered body must struggle without ceasing in order to (not) make the translation" (Moure 2021: 20). Therefore, Moure's intranslatable transelations do not cease to translate, to interpret. They are always in progress, giving voice to all voices. If this is so, the whole process "is of a different order entirely than the familiar and comforting binomes 'fidelity' and 'treason,' 'gain' and 'loss,' 'domesticating' and 'foreignizing'" (Moure 2021: 20).

In women's rewritings the historical traces persist in a different way. They create what Simon calls a "translative impulse," because it introduces "a permanent double consciousness." Perverse translations urge us to listen to all the stories:

> Reading Mouré's transelations, moving from left to right and back, invites us to adopt her doubling habit of mind and everywhere see the gap between one thing and another, between what we see and do not see ... This is the kind of mental event that occurs as a result of perverse translations. The reassurance of an alternate, replacement reality is disturbed by a continuous pulsing of alternatives, the simultaneous awareness of what exists and what could be created from it. (Simon 2006: 154–155)

Moure's citational practices, her palimpsests, her transelations, create "performative translations" (Grass 2023) which involve the whole body:

> Because it involves the body, it is clear to me that translation, and particularly translation of poetry, is a performative gesture, a performance. It is a set of performative gestures implicating the body, performance because the translator does not enact her body as her own but uses her body to perform "the author." (Mouré 2009: 175)

Transelation gives way to a poiesis based on relationality and combines with "the exploration of relationships between poetry and historiography, land and history, the sensorium and language, memory and writing, the dead and the living" (Quéma 2021: 28). Moure is the translator Bassnett describes as writer: the translator who takes that object, dismantles the linguistic signs, and then "composes anew in his or her own language, producing another poem ... The creativity of poet and translator are parallel activities, the only distinction between them being that the poet starts with a blank sheet of paper while the translator starts with the traces of someone else's poem already written" (Bassnett 2014b: 58).

So, these transelations make us reconsider equivalence in translation, the role of the translator and how stories have been written. Transelations are political because they seek to go beyond ordinary communication which she feels perpetuates existing regimes of power. Her poetic and transelative practice seek to subvert what is familiar and to disturb the reader: "It is this that attracts me about translation, that a text in a language unknown to readers in English can perturb and alter English, the comfortable language we inhabit as if it were natural" (Mouré in Williams and Marinkova 2015: 75).

Mouré's intranselations invites us to read in a way that may summarize what women translators intend. Following Deleuze she argues that there are two kinds of readings:

> The first kind of reading is the way reading is taught in classes, in schools, in institutions. The second way of reading is what I call writerly. It finds ways forward or sideways in what the book itself essays; without trying to box it into explanations, it finds ways out of the box. Openings. Curiosities. Glimmers. That's the kind of reading I can best recommend for anyone. Read your way out of the box. Read what you don't already know, plunge in. Read widely across domains and epochs, across intentionality, across languages too, their particular and haunting sounds and formations. You never know how thoughts may come back and re-entwine in the present; thought itself is always haunted by prior or anterior incarnations, by apparent misreadings, by folds and convergences. Even outmoded philosophies can help us read contemporary surfaces and depths in new ways. (Mouré 2009: 15)

What women's translations have shown is that it is possible to find ways forward or sideways. Ways that urge us to read out of the box. Translating as a never-ending process that makes thoughts re-entwine in the present and in the past, thus reading misreadings in new ways again for the first time.

6 (Un)concluding Remarks

The last section of an Element that has approached translation as a never-ending process, always in movement, cannot be conclusive but necessarily open-ended. Women will never stop writing again for the first time the stories already told. All these women writers, translators of the stories already told by what Eduardo Galeano calls the hunters, show that different narratives can be constructed from the same set of records. They also demonstrate that in the twenty-first-century "meaning" is not an easy concept (Malmkjær 2018) and that fidelity and equivalence "are not, of course, simple terms, and have become increasingly relativized in both translation practice and translation studies" (Scott 2011: 215). Translators are "creative agents" (Pernau and Rajamani 2016: 51). Translations are not processes of recalling "but of transmission" and "of reimagination" (Scott 2006/2007: 108) and therefore translation continues to generate powerful representations (Baker 2014) which women in many instances contest and undermine.

Translating is a constant journey between identities; it is continuous movement between spaces, languages, and cultures. Translations are palimpsests,[37] the sound of steps on a street that echo in other streets. Translating means crossing borders, geographical, linguistic, and ideological borders. Translation here "emerges as the central category for the negotiation of difference beyond representation," which means "viewing translation not as a unilateral activity but as a dialogical negotiation – a negotiation, however, that does not need to be harmonious and never takes place outside of power relations" (Pernau and Rajamani 2016: 52). The previous examples have shown how women translate History again for the first time in order to allow new perspectives to be heard. This, no doubt, is not easy and it implies ethics:

> We need stories to give voice to a writer's vision, but also, possibly, to speak for the voiceless. This yearning to hear the voiceless is a powerful rhetoric but also potentially a dangerous one if it prevents us from doing more than listening to a story or reading a book. Just because we have listened to that story or read that book does not mean that anything has changed for the voiceless. Readers and writers should not deceive themselves that literature changes the world. Literature changes the world of readers and writers, but literature does not change the world until people get out of their chairs, go out in the world, and do something to transform the conditions of which the literature speaks. Otherwise literature will just be a fetish for readers and writers, allowing them to think that they are hearing the voiceless when they are really only hearing the writer's individual voice ... That is a writer's dream, that if only we can hear these people that no one else wants to hear, then perhaps we can make you hear them, too. (Nguyen 2018: 12, 14)

Women who translate History also show, as suggested before, that "translation per se is always creative" (Malmkjær 2020: 3), that "translating is not copying" (Malmkjær 2020: 38). As opposed to History conceived as a linear sequence of the development of presence, they show us many different stories

---

[37] The question of palimpsest raised throughout this Element is relevant, not only because of the literary nature of the examples provided here, but also regarding the potential to reflect on palimpsest in history/translation. A few authors have reflected on this topic (e.g., Dilek Dizdar, Rosemary Arrojo, Susan Bassnett, Christopher D. Mellinger, David Johnston, among others). The radical broadening over the last decades of the definition of translation reveals the multiple layering of texts reflecting on the horizontality, nonhierarchical, and pluralistic nature of translation.

conceived as a differentiated and contradictory series. The following step, translating interlinguistically those stories women have previously translated again for the first time, will be a real challenge, since translating will mean here rewriting many voices, layers, palimpsests. As Nguyen states, these translations should be a way to get out of our chairs and go out in the world.

Translating implies here recreating into new materialities. It implies that there is not a single original text but a "previous" text, as Coldiron (2016: 315) states. A very relevant change of perspective, since speaking about a previous text instead of an original means that:

> Every translation is an interpretation, both a rereading and a rewriting: translators deracinate and also resituate the works they re-language, and their actions are neither straightforward in practice nor simple to study ... Translation, in other words, is never reducible to its common definition, "putting a work into another language"; after the cultural turn in translation studies in the 1990s and the current "textual turn," nearly all translation scholarship now acknowledges the many complications that proliferate around an act of translation. But the one consistently accessible site of transformative agency – what we can always hear working through these compounded complexities – is the translator's voice. (Coldiron 2016: 311)

These translations do not offer a general history but rather displaced histories. And, as we travel with women, we realize how important it is for the past to make us hear disturbing cacophonies. Their translations show that

> translation understood in its broadest sense should become a metaphor for transformative thinking about socio-cultural organization ... translation is a means to bring something into the receiving culture ... this process rewrites, that is transforms the source text into something else that belongs to the receiver. Translation is an active agent of change and the translator is the individual who creates that transformation. (Bassnett 2022a: 238)

The way many women writers approach translation is based on difference, not on homogeneity and universalism. Their translations are "necessarily experimental, unable to draw exclusively on the known, begetting knowledge, not meaning" (Scott 2018: 63). Their texts are constantly in movement; they are never stable but unstable, continually reinventable, always "at the text's widening periphery. What do I mean by 'widening periphery'? Through time, through processes of translation, the text fans out into multiple versions of itself, not just interpretations of its meaning, but performances of the experience of reading it" (Scott 2010: 155).

They seek to listen to all the stories contained in the Ocean of the Streams of Story. In these cases, it is "absurd," Bassnett would say, to consider translation as a straightforward activity of substitution. On the contrary, "[t]ranslating a text means reconfiguring it . . . No translation can ever be the 'same' as the original, for translation involves so much more than the linguistic, though obviously language is a crucial element . . . translators have to deal with more than just words which may or may not have dictionary equivalents" (Bassnett 2022c: vii). Women's original stories are translations of previous ones and have the capacity to become new versions of themselves. They manage to join with other stories and to metamorphose into something different. Women's perverse stories are open to plural interpretations and not only limited to those imposed by the hegemonic power of the hunters. They are daring lionesses who write again for the first time stories previously told by men.

References

Adichie, Chimamanda N. 2009. "The Danger of a Single Story," *TED Talks*, July, www.ted.com/talks/chimamanda_adichie_the_danger_of_a_single_story.

Agbabi, Patience. 2018. "Stories in Stanza'd English: A Cross-cultural *Canterbury Tales*," *Literature Compass* 15, 6: e12455, pp. 1–8. https://doi.org/10.1111/lic3.12455.

Agbabi, Patience. 2014. "What Do Women like Bes'? (The Wife of Bath's Tale)," in Oatience Agbabi, ed. *Telling Tales*. Edinburgh: Canongate, 31–37.

Alonzi, Luigi. 2024. "Language – History – Presence," *History and Theory* 63, 3: 366–383.

Alonzi, Luigi. 2023a. "Introduction," in Luigi Alonzi, ed. *History as a Translation of the Past: Case Studies from the West*. London: Bloomsbury Academic, 1–24.

Alonzi, Luigi. 2023b. "The Historian as Translator of the Past," in Luigi Alonzi, ed. *History as a Translation of the Past: Case Studies from the West*. London: Bloomsbury Academic, 191–213.

Alonzi, Luigi. 2023c. "History as Translation/Anachronism as Synchronism," *Rethinking History* 27, 4: 664–683.

Altman, Toby. 2022. "'What Beauty Was': Jen Bervin's Untimely Sonnets," *ELH* 89, 2: 489–522.

Altman, Toby. 2021. "Silk Poetics (on Jen Bervin's Silk Poems and Aditi Machado's *Emporium* and *The End*)," *The Georgia Review*, Fall, www.thegeorgiareview.com/posts/silk-poetics-on-jen-bervins-silk-poems-and-aditi-machados-emporium-and-the-end/.

Altman, Toby. 2020. "Caroline Bergvall, *Alisoun Sings*," *Chicago Review*, Autumn, n.p.

Bacchilega, Cristina. 2018. "Postmodernism," in Pauline Greenhill, Jill Terry Rudy, Naomi Hamer, and Lauren Bosc, eds. *The Routledge Companion to Media and Fairy-Tale Cultures*. London: Routledge, 74–90.

Bacchilega, Cristina. 2013. *Fairy Tales Transformed? Twenty-First-Century Adaptations and the Politics of Wonder*. Detroit: Wayne State University Press.

Bacchilega, Cristina. 1997. *Postmodern Fairy Tales: Gender and Narrative Strategies*. Pennsylvania: University of Pennsylvania.

Bacchilega, Cristina, and Jennifer Orme, eds. 2021. *Inviting Interruptions: Wonder Tales in the 21st Century*. Detroit: Wayne State University Press.

Baer, Brian J. 2020. "On Origins: The Mythistory of Translation Studies and the Geopolitics of Knowledge," *The Translator* 26, 3: 221–240.

Baker, Mona, ed. 2016. *Translating Dissent*. London: Routledge.

Baker, Mona. 2014. "The Changing Landscape of Translation and Interpreting Studies," in Sandra Bermann and Catherine Porter, eds. *A Companion to Translation Studies*. Oxford: Wiley-Blackwell, 15–24.

Baker, Mona. 2006. *Translation and Conflict: A Narrative Account*. London: Routledge.

Bal, Mieke. 2009. *Narratology: Introduction to the Theory of Narrative*. Toronto: University of Toronto Press.

Barnes, Julian. 1989. *A History of the World in 10 ½ Chapters*. New York: Alfred A. Knopf.

Barthes, Roland. 1967/1989. "The Discourse of History", in *The Rustle of Language*. New York: Hill and Wang, 127–140. Trans. Richard Howard.

Bassnett, Susan. 2022a. "Translation, Transcreation, Transgression," in Laura Jansen, ed. *Anne Carson: Antiquity*. London: Bloomsbury, 237–250.

Bassnett, Susan. 2022b. "Beyond Faithfulness: Retranslating Classic Texts," in Jan Steyn, ed. *Translation: Crafts, Contexts, Consequences*. Cambridge: Cambridge University Press, 112–125.

Bassnett, Susan. 2022c. "Preface" to Mª Carmen África Vidal Claramonte, *Translation and Contemporary Art: Transdisciplinary Encounters*. New York and London: Routledge, vii–xi.

Bassnett, Susan. 2014a. *Translation*. London and New York: Routledge.

Bassnett, Susan. 2014b. "Variations on Translation," in Sandra Bermann and Catherine Porter, eds. *A Companion to Translation Studies*. Chichester: Wiley Blackwell, 54–66.

Bassnett, Susan. 2006/2007. "Writing and Translating," in Susan Bassnett and Peter Bush, eds. *The Translator as Writer*. London: Continuum, 173–183.

Beckett, Sandra L. 2013. *Revisioning Red Riding Hood around the World: An Anthology of International Retellings*. Detroit: Wayne State University Press.

Bergvall, Caroline. 2019. *Alisoun Sings*. New York: Nightboat Books.

Bergvall, Caroline. 2010. *Middling English*. Southampton: John Hansard Gallery.

Bernheimer, Kate, ed. 2010. *My Mother She Killed Me, My Father He Ate Me: Forty New Fairy Tales*. New York: Penguin.

Bernheimer, Kate, ed. 2007. *Brothers and Beasts: An Anthology of Men on Fairy Tales*. Detroit: Wayne State University Press.

Bernheimer, Kate, ed. 1998. *Mirror, Mirror on the Wall: Women Writers Explore Their Favourite Fairy Tales*. New York: Anchor Books.

Bernstein, Lisa. 2020. "Translating History into Herstories: Utopian Impulses in the Dystopian Worlds of Christa Wolf and Carmen Boullosa," in Norbert Bachleitner, ed. *Volume 2 Literary Translation, Reception, and Transfer.* Berlin: De Gruyter, 225–235.

Bervin, Jen. 2004/2019. *Nets.* Brooklyn: Ugly Duckling Press.

Bielsa, Esperanza. 2006. *The Latin American Urban Crónica: Between Literature and Mass Culture.* Oxford: Lexington.

Borodo, Michal, and Jorge Díaz-Cintas, eds. 2025. *The Routledge Handbook of Translation and Young Audiences.* London: Routledge.

Braz, Albert. 2009. "Correcting the Master: Erin Mouré, Alberto Caeiro, and the Politics of 'Transelation'," *Graphos: João Pessoa* 11, 2, December: 64–72.

Broqua, Vincent. 2010. "Living-with Shakespeare? (Three American Experimental Poets' Compositions with Shakespeare's Sonnet 130)," *Transatlantica. Revue d'études américaines: American Studies Journal* 1: 1–16.

Bryman, Alan. 2004. *The Disneyization of Society.* London: SAGE.

Burke, Peter. 2005. "Lost (and Found) in Translation: A Cultural History of Translators and Translating in Early Modern Europe," *NIAS*, Amsterdam [online]. https://nias.knaw.nl/wp-content/uploads/2018/01/KB_01_Peter-Burke.pdf.

Carney, Jo Eldridge. 2022. *Women Talk Back to Shakespeare: Contemporary Adaptations and Appropriations.* London: Routledge.

Carson, Anne. 2013. *Nay Rather.* Paris: The Cahiers Series. Sylph Editions.

Carter, Angela. 2000. "Polemical preface: Pornography in the Service of Women," in Drucilla Cornell, ed. *Oxford Readings in Feminism: Feminism and Pornography.* Oxford: Oxford University Press.

Carter, Angela. 1983. "Notes from the Front Line," in Lindsey Tucker, ed. *Critical Essays on Angela Carter.* New York: G. K. Hall, 24–30.

Castro, Olga, and María Laura Spoturno. 2021. "How Rebel Can Translation Be? A (Con)textual Study of *Good Night Stories for Rebel Girls* and Two Translations into Spanish", in Maud Anne Bracke, Julia C. Bullock, Penelope Morris, and Kristina Schulz, eds. *Translating Feminism: Interdisciplinary Approaches to Text, Place and Agency.* New York: Palgrave Macmillan, 227–256.

Chakrabarty, Dipesh. 2002. *Habitations of Modernity: Essays in the Wake of Subaltern Studies.* Chicago: The University of Chicago Press.

Cheung, Martha. 2012. "The Mediated Nature of Knowledge and the Pushing-hands Approach to Research on Translation History," *Translation Studies* 5, 2: 156–171.

Coldiron, Anne E. B. 2016. "Introduction: Beyond Babel, or, the Agency of Translators in Early Modern Literature and History," *Philological Quarterly* 95, 3/4: 311–323.

Coldiron, Anne E. B. 2012. "Visibility Now: Historicizing Foreign Presences in Translation," *Translation Studies* 5, 2: 189–200.

Coppola, Manuela. 2015. "A Tale of Two Wives: The Transnational Poetry of Patience Agbabi and Jean 'Binta' Breeze," *Journal of Postcolonial Writing* 52, 3: 305–318. https://doi.org/10.1080/17449855.2015.1091373.

Cronin, Michael. 2007. "Double Take: Figuring the Other and the Politics of Translation," in Paul St-Pierre and Prafulla C. Kar, eds. *In Translation – Reflections, Refractions, Transformations*. Amsterdam: John Benjamins, 253–262.

D'Arcens, Louise. 2021. *World Medievalism: The Middle Ages in Modern Textual Culture*. Oxford: Oxford University Press.

Daly, Niki. 2007. *Pretty Salma: A Little Red Riding Hood Story from Africa*. New York: Clarion Books.

Daré, Abi. 2020. *The Girl with the Louding Voice*. London: Hodder and Stoughton.

De Certeau, Michel. 1975/1988. *The Writing of History*. New York: Columbia University Press.

Deane-Cox, Sharon. 2016. *Retranslation: Translation, Literature and Reinterpretation*. London: Bloomsbury Academic.

Dworkin, Andrea. 1974. *Woman Hating*. New York: Dutton.

Estrada, Carmen. 2021. *Odiseicas: Las mujeres en la Odisea*. Barcelona: Seix Barral.

Feder, Rachel, and Tiffany Tatreau. 2024. *Taylor Swift by the Book: The Literature behind the Lyrics, from Fairy Tales to Tortured Poets*. Philadelphia: Quirk Books.

Fiander, Lisa M. 2004. *Fairy Tales and the Fiction of Iris Murdoch, Margaret Drabble, and A. S. Byatt*. Frankfurt: Peter Lang.

Foucault, Michel. 1970/1981. "The Order of Discourse", in Robert Young, ed. *Untying the Text: A Post-Structuralist Reader*. London: Routledge, 48–78. Trans. Ian McLeod.

Galeano, Eduardo. 1989/1992. *The Book of Embraces*. New York: W. W. Norton. Trans. Cedric Belfrage.

Garland, Carina. 2008. "Curious Appetites: Food, Desire, Gender, and Subjectivity in Lewis Carroll's Alice Texts," *The Lion and the Unicorn* 32, 1: 22–39.

Gilbert, Sandra M., and Susan Gubar. 2000. *The Madwoman in the Attic: The Woman Writer and the Nineteenth-century Literary Imagination*. New Haven: Yale University Press.

Gold, Alexandra C. 2019. "At Will: The Queer Possibility of Jen Bervin's *Nets*," *Contemporary Women's Writing* 13, 1: 89–106.

Goldsmith, Kenneth. 2011. *Uncreative Writing: Managing Language in the Digital Age*. New York: Columbia University Press.

Grass, Delphine. 2023. *Translation as Creative – Critical Practice*. Cambridge: Cambridge University Press.

Greene, Gayle. 1991. "Feminist Fiction and the Uses of Memory," *Signs* 16, 2: 290–321.

Greenhill, Pauline, Jill Terry Rudy, Naomi Hamer, and Lauren Bosc, eds. 2018. *Routledge Companion to Media and Fairy-Tale Cultures*. London: Routledge.

Guha, Ranajit, ed. 1997. *A Subaltern Studies Reader 1986–1995*. Minneapolis: University of Minnesota Press.

Guran, Paula. ed. 2016. *Beyond the Woods: Fairy Tales Retold*. Jersey City: Night Shade Books.

Guran, Paula, ed. 2013. *Once Upon a Time: New Fairy Tales*. Gaithersburg: Prime Books.

Haase, Donald. 2016. "Challenges of Folktale and Fairy-Tale Studies in the Twenty-First Century," *Fabula* 57, 1–2: 73–85.

Haase, Donald. 2010. "Decolonizing Fairy-Tale Studies," *Marvels & Tales* 24: 17–38.

Haase, Donald, ed. 2004. *Fairy Tales and Feminism: New Approaches*. Detroit: Wayne State University Press.

Harding, Sue-Ann. 2022a. "Narratology and Narrative Theory," in Christopher Rundle, ed. *The Routledge Handbook of Translation History*. London: Routledge, 54–69.

Harding, Sue-Ann. 2022b. "Translating Collective Memory of Beslan: Russian State Television News Coverage of Annual Commemorations and Narratives of Silence, Othering, Separation and Abstraction," in Sharon Deane-Cox and Anneleen Spiessens, eds. *The Routledge Handbook of Translation and Memory*. London: Routledge, 42–57.

Harding, Sue-Ann. 2012. *Beslan: Six Stories of the Siege*. Manchester: Manchester University Press.

Harries, Elizabeth W. 2001. *Twice Upon a Time: Women Writers and the History of the Fairy Tale*. Princeton: Princeton University Press.

Hennard Dutheil de la Rochère, Martine. 2019. "Translation, Illustration, Transcreation: From the Fairy Tales of Charles Perrault to Classic Fairy Tales Retold," *Études de lettres*, 310: 59–80.

Hennard Dutheil de la Rochère, Martine. 2013. *Reading, Translating, Rewriting: Angela Carter's Translational Poetics*. Detroit: Wayne State University Press.

Hennard Dutheil de la Rochere, Martine, Gillian Lathey, and Monika Woźniak, eds. 2016. *Cinderella across Cultures: New Directions and Interdisciplinary Perspectives*. Detroit: Wayne State University Press.

Hermans, Theo. 2022. *Translation and History: A Textbook*. London: Routledge.

Holliday, Christopher. 2019. "Let It Go? Towards a 'Plasmatic' Perspective on Digital Disney," in Amy A. Davis, ed. *Discussing Disney*. New Barnet: John Libbey, pp. 115–136.

hooks, bell. 1991. "Talking Back," in Russell Ferguson et al., eds. *Out There: Marginalization and Contemporary Cultures*. New York: The MIT Press, 337–344.

hoʻomanawanui, kuʻualoha. 2018. "Indigeneity. *E Hoʻokikohoʻe iā Peʻapeʻamakawalu* (Digitizing the Eight-Eyed Bat): Indigenous Wonder Tales, Culture, and Media," in Pauline Greenhill, Jill Terry Rudy, Naomi Hamer, and Lauren Bosc, eds. *The Routledge Companion to Media and Fairy-Tale Cultures*. London: Routledge, 122–132.

Hutcheon, Linda. 1989. *The Politics of Postmodernism*. New York: Routledge.

Hutcheon, Linda. 1988. *A Poetics of Postmodernism: History, Theory, Fiction*. New York: Routledge.

Jardine, Alice. 1985. *Gynesis: Configurations of Woman and Modernity*. Ithaca: Cornell University Press.

Jenkins, Keith. 1991/2003. *Re-thinking History*. New York: Routledge.

Joosen, Vanessa. 2011. *Critical and Creative Perspectives on Fairy Tales: An Intertextual Dialogue between Fairy-Tale Scholarship and Postmodern Retellings*. Detroit: Wayne State University Press.

Jörgensen, Beth E. 1994. *The Writing of Elena Poniatowska: Engaging Dialogues*. Austin: University of Texas Press.

Karpinski, Eva C. 2012. *Borrowed Tongues: Life, Writing, Migration, and Translation*. Waterloo: Wilfrid Laurier University Press.

Kérchy, Anna, ed. 2011. *Postmodern Reinterpretations of Fairy Tales: How Applying New Methods Generates New Meanings*. Lewiston: The Edwin Mellen Press.

Knowles, Murray, and Kirsten Malmkjær. 1996. *Language and Control in Children's Literature*. London: Routledge.

Koselleck, Reinhart. 2002. *The Practice of Conceptual History: Timing History, Spacing Concepts*. Stanford: Stanford University Press.

Kostelanetz, Richard. 2019. *A Dictionary of the Avant-Gardes*. London: Routledge.

LaCapra, Dominick. 2013. *History, Literature, Critical Theory*. Ithaca: Cornell University Press.

LaCapra, Dominick. 2004. *History in Transit: Experience, Identity, Critical Theory*. Ithaca: Cornell University Press.

LaCapra, Dominick. 1985. *History and Criticism*. Ithaca: Cornell University Press.

LaCapra, Dominick. 1983/1994. *Rethinking Intellectual History: Texts, Contexts, Language*. Ithaca: Cornell University Press.

Leduc, Amanda. 2020. *Disfigured: On Fairy Tales, Disability, and Making Space*. Ontario: Canada Council of Arts.

Lefevere, André. 1988. "Holy Garbage, tho' by Homer cook't," *Traduction, Terminologie, Redaction* 1, 2: 19–27.

Lieberman, Marcia R. 1972. "Some Day My Prince Will Come': Female Acculturation through the Fairy Tale", College English 34, 3, December: 383–395.

Maguire, Shannon. 2015. "Parasite Poetics: Noise and Queer Hospitality in Erín Moure's *O Cidadán*," *Canadian Literature* 224, Spring: 47–63.

Malmkjær, Kirsten. 2022. "Introduction," in Kirsten Malmkjær, ed. *The Cambridge Handbook of Translation*. Cambridge: Cambridge University Press, 1–9.

Malmkjær, Kirsten. 2020. *Translation and Creativity*. New York: Routledge.

Malmkjær, Kirsten. 2018. "Semantics and Translation," in Kirsten Malmkjær, ed. *The Routledge Handbook of Translation Studies and Linguistics*. London: Routledge, 31–44.

Marczewska, Kaja. 2018. *This Is Not a Copy: Writing at the Iterative Turn*. New York: Bloomsbury.

Mellinger, Christopher D., and Thomas A. Hanson. 2022. "Research Data," in Federico Zanettin, Christopher Rundle eds. *The Routledge Handbook of Translation and Methodology*. London: Routledge, 307–323.

Miles, Rosalind. 1988/2001. *Who Cooked the Last Supper? The Women's History of the World*. New York: Three Rivers Press.

Mohanty, Chandra Talpade. 1991. "Cartographies of Struggle: Third World Women and the Politics of Feminism," in Chandra Talpade Mohanty, Ann Russo, and Lourdes Torres, eds. *Third World Women and the Politics of Feminism*. Bloomington: Indiana University Press, 1–47.

Morley, Neville. 1999/2002. *Writing Ancient History*. London: Duckworth.

Moure, Erín. 2021. "Elisa Sampedrín and the Paradox of Translation, or the Intranslatable," *Zat-So Productions*. https://erinmoure.mystrikingly.com/#es-and-the-paradox-of-translation-or-the-intranslatable-pdf.

Moure, Erín. 2009. *My Beloved Wager: Essays from a Writing Practice*. Alberta: NeWest Press.

Moure, Eirin. 2001. *Sheep's Vigil by a Fervent Person, A Transelation of Alberto Caeiro/Fernando Pessoa's O Guardador de Rebanhos*. Toronto: House of Anansi.

Munslow, Alun, ed. 2013. *Authoring the Past: Writing and Rethinking History*. London: Routledge.

Munslow, Alun. 2012. *A History of History*. London: Routledge.

Munslow, Alun. 1997. *Deconstructing History*. London: Routledge.

Ngaba, Buhle. 2019. *The Girl Without a Sound*. London: Central Books.

Nguyen, Viet Thanh, ed. 2018. *The Displaced: Refugee Writers on Refugee Lives*. New York: Abrams Press.

Nissan, Greg. 2019. "Terms of Exchange: Caroline Bergvall Interviewed," *Bomb*, December 13, n.p. https://bombmagazine.org/articles/2019/12/13/caroline-bergvall/.

Olsen, Niklas. 2014. *History in the Plural: An Introduction to the Work of Reinhart Koselleck*. New York: Berghahn.

Orwell, George. 1949/1983. *Nineteen Eighty-Four*. Harmondsworth: Penguin.

Owens, Craig. 1983. "The Discourse of Others: Feminists and Postmodernism", in Hal Foster, ed. *The Anti-Aesthetic: Essays on Postmodern Culture*. Seattle: Bay Press, 57–82.

Owens, Richard. 2015. "Caroline Bergvall her 'Shorter Chaucer Tales'," *Postmedieval: A Journal of Medieval Cultural Studies* 6, 146–153.

Parrish, Rhonda, ed. 2021. *Clockwork, Curses, and Coal: Steampunk and Gaslamp Fairy Tales*. Michigan: World Weaver Press.

Parrish, Rhonda, ed. 2019. *Grimm, Grit, and Gasoline: Dieselpunk and Decopunk Fairy Tales*. Michigan: World Weaver Press.

Pernau, Margrit, and Imke Rajamani. 2016. "Emotional Translations: Conceptual History Beyond Language," *History and Theory* 55, February: 46–65.

Philip, M. NourbeSe. 2018. "The Ga(s)p," in Myung Mi Kim and Cristanne Miller, eds. *Poetics and Precarity*. Albany: State University of New York Press, 31–40.

Pillière, Linda, and Özlem Berk Albachten, eds. 2024. *The Routledge Handbook of Intralingual Translation*. New York and London: Routledge.

Polezzi, Loredana. 2020. "From Substitution to Co-presence: Translation, Memory and Trace in the Visual Practices of Diasporic Italian Artists," in

Charles Burdett, Loredana Polezzi, and Barbara Spadaro, eds. *Transcultural Italies: Mobility, Memory and Translation*. Liverpool: Liverpool University Press, pp. 317–340.

Price, Patricia L. 2004. *Dry Place: Landscapes of Belonging and Exclusion*. Minneapolis: University of Minnesota Press.

Pulliam, Amy. 2025. "When a Fairy Tale Yields More than a Moral: Illuminating Immigrant Literature Themes through Diverse Versions of Little Red Riding Hood," *Literacy Practice and Research* 49, 2, Article 1. https://digitalcommons.fiu.edu/lpr/vol49/iss2/1.

Quéma, Anne. 2021. "Bioarchives of Affect: Erín Moure's *The Unmemntioable*," *Studies in Canadian Literature*, 45, 2: 25–47.

Ray, Shakuntala. 2022. "Profane Cooks and Minor Condiments: Chutnification and 'cooking the world' in Salman Rushdie's *Midnight's Children*," *The Journal of Commonwealth Literature* 57, 1: 64–82.

Rich, Adrienne. 1972. "When We Dead Awaken: Writing as Re-Vision," *College English*, 34, 1, October: 18–30.

Robert-Foley, Lily. 2024. *Experimental Translation: The Work of Translation in the Age of Algorithmic Production*. London: Goldsmiths Press.

Robinson, Douglas. 2022. *The Experimental Translator*. Cham: Palgrave Macmillan.

Rundle, Christopher. 2020. "Historiography," in Mona Baker and Gabriela Saldanha, eds. *Routledge Encyclopedia of Translation Studies*. 3rd ed. London: Routledge, 232–237.

Rundle, Christopher. 2012. "Translation as an Approach to History," *Translation Studies* 5, 2: 232–240.

Rundle, Christopher, and Vicente Rafael. 2016. "History and Translation: The Event of Language," in Yves Gambier and Luc van Doorslaer, eds. *Border Crossings: Translation Studies and Other Disciplines*. Amsterdam: John Benjamins, 23–48.

Rushdie, Salman. 1997. "Notes on Writing and the Nation," *Index on Censorship* 26, 3: 34–39.

Rushdie, Salman. 1990/1999. *Haroun and the Sea of Stories*. London: Granta.

Rushdie, Salman. 1981/1995. *Midnight's Children*. London: Vintage.

Rushdie, Salman. 2019. *Quichotte: A Novel*. New York: Random House.

Scott, Clive. 2019. "Synaesthesia and Intersemiosis: Competing Principles in Literary Translation," in Madeleine Campbell and Ricarda Vidal, eds. *Translating across Sensory and Linguistic Borders: Intersemiotic Journeys between Media*. New York: Palgrave Macmillan, 87–112.

Scott, Clive. 2018. *The Work of Literary Translation*. Cambridge: Cambridge University Press.

Scott, Clive. 2011. "The Translation of Reading: A Phenomenological Approach," *Translation Studies* 4, 2: 213–229.

Scott, Clive. 2010. "Intermediality and Synesthesia: Literary Translation as Centrifugal Practice," *Art in Translation* 2, 2: 153–169.

Scott, Clive. 2009. "From Linearity to Tabularity," *CTIS Occasional Papers*, vol. 4. Manchester: The University of Manchester, 37–53.

Scott, Clive. 2006/2007. "Translating the Literary: Genetic Criticism, Text Theory and Poetry," in Susan Bassnett and Peter Bush, eds. *The Translator as Writer*. London: Continuum, 105–118.

Shi, Flair Donglai. 2016. "*Alice's Adventures in Wonderland* as an Anti-Feminist Text: Historical, Psychoanalytical and Postcolonial Perspectives," *Women: A Cultural Review* 27, 2: 177–201.

Simon, Sherry. 2006. *Translating Montreal: Episodes in the Life of a Divided City*. Montreal: McGill-Queen's University Press.

Simon, Sherry. 2007. "A Single Brushstroke: Writing through Translation: Anne Carson," in Paul St-Pierre and Prafulla C. Kar, eds. *In Translation – Reflections, Refractions, Transformations*. Amsterdam: John Benjamins, 107–116.

Slack-Smith, Amanda. 2018. "Contemporary Art," in Pauline Greenhill, Jill Terry Rudy, Naomi Hamer, and Lauren Bosc, eds. *The Routledge Companion to Media and Fairy-Tale Cultures*. London: Routledge, 492–500.

Sohár, Anikó. 2019. "Fairy Tales Retold in Words and Pictures," *Translation Matters* 1, 2: 9–29.

Spivak, Gayatri Chakravorty. 1993/1996. "Bonding in Difference: Interview with Alfred Arteaga," in Donna Landry and Gerald MacLean, eds. *The Spivak Reader*. London: Routledge, 15–28.

Spivak, Gayatri Chakravorty. 1985. "Subaltern Studies: Deconstructing Historiography," in Ranajit Guha, ed. *Subaltern Studies IV*. New Delhi: Oxford University Press, 330–363.

Spivak, Gayatri Chakravorty. 1990. *The Post-Colonial Critic. Interviews, Strategies, Dialogues*. New York: Routledge.

St-Pierre, Paul. 2012. "Response," *Translation Studies* 5, 2: 240–242.

St-Pierre, Paul. 1993. "Translation as a Discourse of History," *TTR: Traduction, Terminologie, Rédaction* 6, 1: 61–82.

Swift, Graham. 1983. *Waterland*. London: Heinemann.

Tatar, Maria. 2020. *The Fairest of Them All: Snow White and 21 Tales of Mothers and Daughters*. Cambridge: The Belknap Press of Harvard University Press.

Tatar, Maria, ed. 2015. *The Cambridge Companion to Fairy Tales*. Cambridge: Cambridge University Press.

References

Tatar, Maria. 1992. *Off with Their Heads! Fairytales and the Culture of Childhood*. Princeton: Princeton University Press.

Tatar, Maria. 1987/2019. *The Hard Facts of the Grimms' Fairy Tales*. Princeton: Princeton University Press.

Teverson, Andrew, ed. 2019. *The Fairy Tale World*. London: Routledge.

Trouillot, Michel-Rolph. 1995. *Silencing the Past: Power and the Production of History*. Boston: Beacon Press.

Turner, Marion. 2023. *The Wife of Bath: A Biography*. Princeton: Princeton University Press.

Vidal Claramonte, Mª Carmen África. 2025. "Translating Fairytales through Women's Bodies: From Cindy Sherman to Dina Goldstein," in Madeleine Campbell and Ricarda Vidal, eds. *The Translation of Experience*. London: Routledge, 170–191.

Vidal Claramonte, Mª Carmen África. 2023. "Translating Invisible Lives: Paul Bowles' Rewritings of His Moroccan Storytellers," *Mutatis Mutandis: Revista Latinoamericana de Traducción* 16, 1: 65–83.

Wang, Caroline Yiqian. 2025. "Re-Imaging Empowered Princesshood against the Rise of the Fourth-Wave Feminism: A Thematic Study of Disney's Princess Live-Action Remakes," *International Journal of Disney Studies* 1, 1: 33–51.

Warner, Marina. 2014. *Once Upon a Time: A Short History of Fairy Tale*. Oxford: Oxford University Press.

Warner, Marina. 1995. *From the Beast to the Blonde: Fairy Tales and Their Tellers*. London: Vintage.

Whelan, Bridget. 2014. "Power to the Princess: Disney and the Creation of the Twentieth Century Princess Narrative," in Alexander N. Howe and Wynn Yarbrough, eds. *Kidding around: The Child in Film and Media*. New York: Bloomsbury, 167–191.

White, Hayden. 1987. *The Content of the Form: Narrative Discourse and Historical Representation*. Baltimore: The Johns Hopkins University Press.

White, Hayden. 1978a. *Tropics of Discourse: Essays in Cultural Criticism*. Baltimore: Johns Hopkins University Press.

White, Hayden. 1978b. "The Historical Text as Literary Artifact," in Robert H. Canary and Henry Kozicki, eds. *The Writing of History*. Wisconsin: The University of Wisconsin Press, 41–62.

White, Hayden. 1975. *Metahistory*. Baltimore: Johns Hopkins University Press.

Williams, Dominic, and Milena Marinkova. 2015. "Affective Trans-scapes: Affect, Translation, and Landscape in Erín Moure's *The Unmentionable*," *Contemporary Women's Writing* 9, 1: 73–92.

Wilson, Rita, and Leah Gerber. 2012. "Introduction," in Rita Wilson and Leah Gerber, eds. *Creative Constraints: Translation and Authorship.* Monash: Monash University Publishing, ix–xv.

Wright, Katheryn. 2016. *The New Heroines: Female Embodiment and Technology in 21st-Century Popular Culture.* Santa Barabara: Praeger.

Young, Robert. 1990. *White Mythologies: Writing History and the West.* London: Routledge.

Zipes, Jack. 2011. *The Enchanted Screen: The Unknown History of Fairy-Tale Films.* London: Routledge.

Zipes, Jack. 2008. "Introduction", in Angela Carter, *The Fairy Tales of Charles Perrault.* New York: Penguin.

Zipes, Jack. 2001. *Sticks and Stones: The Troublesome Success of Children's Literature from Slovenly Peter to Harry Potter.* New York: Routledge.

Zipes, Jack, ed. 2000. *The Oxford Companion to Fairy Tales: The Western Fairy Tale Tradition from Medieval to Modern.* Oxford: Oxford University Press.

Zipes, Jack, ed. 1986. *Don't Bet on the Prince: Contemporary Feminist Fairy Tales in North America and England.* New York: Methuen.

Acknowledgments

I would like to express my deepest gratitude to my editor, Kirsten Malmkjær, whose wise suggestions have improved the original manuscript and whose professionalism, generosity, patience, and kindness have greatly facilitated the publication of this Element.

Cambridge Elements

Translation and Interpreting

The series is edited by Kirsten Malmkjær with Sabine Braun as associate editor for Elements focusing on Interpreting.

Kirsten Malmkjær
University of Leicester

Kirsten Malmkjær is Professor Emeritus of Translation Studies at the University of Leicester. She has taught Translation Studies at the universities of Birmingham, Cambridge, Middlesex and Leicester and has written extensively on aspects of both the theory and practice of the discipline. *Translation and Creativity* (London: Routledge) was published in 2020 and *The Cambridge Handbook of Translation*, which she edited, was published in 2022. She is preparing a volume entitled *Introducing Translation* for the Cambridge Introductions to Language and Linguistics series.

Editorial Board
Adriana Serban, *Université Paul Valéry*
Barbara Ahrens, *Technische Hochschule Köln*
Liu Min-Hua, *Hong Kong Baptist University*
Christine Ji, *The University of Sydney*
Jieun Lee, *Ewha Womans University*
Lorraine Leeson, *The University of Dublin*
Sara Laviosa, *Università Delgi Stuidi di Bari Aldo Moro*
Fabio Alves, *FALE-UFMG*
Moira Inghilleri, *University of Massachusetts Amherst*
Akiko Sakamoto, *University of Portsmouth*
Haidee Kotze, *Utrecht University*

About the Series
Elements in Translation and Interpreting present cutting edge studies on the theory, practice and pedagogy of translation and interpreting. The series also features work on machine learning and AI, and human-machine interaction, exploring how they relate to multilingual societies with varying communication and accessibility needs, as well as text-focused research.

Cambridge Elements

Translation and Interpreting

Elements in the Series

The Graeco-Arabic Translation Movement
El-Hussein AY Aly

Interpreting as Translanguaging: Theory, Research, and Practice
Lili Han, Zhisheng (Edward) Wen and Alan James Runcieman

Creative Classical Translation
Paschalis Nikolaou

Translation as Creative–Critical Practice
Delphine Grass

Translation in Analytic Philosophy
Francesca Ervas

Towards Game Translation User Research
Mikołaj Deckert, Krzysztof W. Hejduk, and Miguel Ángel Bernal-Merino

An Extraordinary Chinese Translation of Holocaust Testimony
Meiyuan Zhao

Hypertranslation
Mª África Vidal Claramonte and Tong King Lee

Researching and Modelling the Translation Process
Muhammad M. M. Abdel Latif

Risk Management in Translation
Anthony Pym

Literary Exophonic Translation
Lúcia Collischonn

Translating His-stories
Mª Carmen África Vidal Claramonte

A full series listing is available at: www.cambridge.org/EITI

For EU product safety concerns, contact us at Calle de José Abascal, 56–1°,
28003 Madrid, Spain or eugpsr@cambridge.org.